George Orwell Studies

Volume Two

No. 1

George Orwell Studies

Publishing Office
Abramis Academic
ASK House
Northgate Avenue
Bury St. Edmunds
Suffolk
IP32 6BB
UK

Tel: +44 (0)1284 700321
Fax: +44 (0)1284 717889
Email: info@abramis.co.uk
Web: www.abramis.co.uk

Copyright
All rights reserved. No part of this publication may be reproduced in any material form (including photocopying or storing it in any medium by electronic means, and whether or not transiently or incidentally to some other use of this publication) without the written permission of the copyright owner, except in accordance with the provisions of the Copyright, Designs and Patents Act 1988, or under terms of a licence issued by the Copyright Licensing Agency Ltd, 33-34, Alfred Place, London WC1E 7DP, UK. Applications for the copyright owner's permission to reproduce part of this publication should be addressed to the Publishers.

© 2017 George Orwell Studies & Abramis Academic

ISSN 2399-1267
ISBN 978-1-84549-717-0

George Orwell

Contents

Editorial
Why Orwell Matters to Teachers Today – by Tim Crook — Page 3

Special Section 1: Teaching Orwell
Papers
George Orwell versus Vera Brittain: Obliteration Bombing and the Tolerance in Wartime of Dissent in Weekly Political Publications – by Tim Luckhurst and Lesley Phippen — Page 6

Big Brother is Coming to an iPad Near You: Teaching Orwell in Taiwan – by Henk Vynckier — Page 21

Orwell the Teacher: Such, Such Were the Joys – by Tim Crook — Page 38

Articles
Orwell's Children: Fighting for Voice – by Jon Preston — Page 52

The Rhetoric of Doublethink – by Philip Palmer — Page 61

A Short History of Hate – by Sean Cubitt — Page 69

Special Section 2: Orwell and Labour
edited by John Newsinger

Orwell, the Labour Party and the Attlee Government – by John Newsinger — Page 78

Leaders and their Qualities: Orwell on Cripps, Bevan and Attlee – by Philip Bounds — Page 88

So What Kind of Democratic Socialist Was He? – by Paul Anderson — Page 97

Plus
The Orwell Conundrum in *Coming Up for Air*: A Call for Action or Passive Resistance? – by Oriol Quintana — Page 112

Death, Hegemony and Masks: Reimaging Theories of Resistance Through the Writings of George Orwell – by Harry Bark — Page 122

Reviews
Peter Stansky on *Churchill & Orwell: The Fight for Freedom*, by Thomas E. Ricks; Douglas Kerr on *George Orwell and Religion*, by Michael G. Brennan; Richard Lance Keeble on *We Know All About You: The Story of Surveillance in Britain and America*, by Rhodri Jeffreys-Jones; Nick Crowson on *Incognito Social Investigation in British Literature: Certainties in Degradation*, by Luke Seaber — Page 136

Editors
John Newsinger — Bath Spa University
Richard Lance Keeble — University of Lincoln

Reviews Editor
Luke Seaber — University College London

Production Editor
Paul Anderson — University of Essex

Editorial Board
Kristin Bluemel — Monmouth University, New Jersey
Tim Crook — Goldsmiths, University of London
Peter Marks — University of Sydney
Marina Remy — Paris Sorbonne
Jean Seaton — University of Westminster
Peter Stansky — Stanford University, US
D. J. Taylor — Author, journalist, biographer of Orwell
Florian Zollmann — Newcastle University

EDITORIAL

Why Orwell Matters to Teachers Today

TIM CROOK

The second George Orwell Studies conference at Goldsmiths, University of London, in June 2017 focused on the theme of 'Teaching Orwell' in a year when sales of *Animal Farm* and *Nineteen Eighty Four* experienced peaks of demand following the election of US President Donald Trump. As expressions such as 'alternative facts', 'post truth' and 'fake news' have entered the everyday lexicon of political discussion and journalistic coverage, we have been reminded that Orwell's famous novels are the mainstays of literary studies curricula throughout the world.

Orwell had strong views on the nature of teaching, his experience of it as a child and, during the two years leading up to the publication of his first book in 1933, tried his hand at school mastering at two private schools in Hayes and Uxbridge in West London. At the Hawthornes, in Hayes, Orwell told a friend he 'was living in a sort of nightmare – schoolwork, rehearsing boys for their parts in the play, making costumes, & playing football … I don't find the work uninteresting, but it is very exhausting…' (Meyers 2001: 98). At a second co-educational school in nearby Uxbridge, he taught by day, wrote by night and developed pneumonia after getting completely soaked riding his motorbike in the freezing rain. He was too weak to continue his teaching career and, like D. H. Lawrence, 'was permanently released from that dead-end job by illness' (ibid: 100).

This also marked an intriguing transition between his real-life identity as Eric Arthur Blair to the authorial pseudonym of 'George Orwell'. Were they one and the same person or did he become a bifurcation of two personalities activating, reporting on and fictionalising each other's interior and external journeys? Orwell wrote essays and novels that were heavily critical and satirical of teachers and the system they worked in. In 'Such, Such Were the Joys', Orwell let rip on all of the slights and humiliations he experienced as a child at St. Cyprian's, his Eastbourne preparatory school, that burned down with the death of a servant girl in 1939. He said he 'was relatively happy' at Eton, but avoided school reunions and old boys' dinners.

Orwell tackled education as one of those shabby, for-profit rackets that denied social justice. He was symbolically and creatively on the side of childhood sensibility. As far as he was concerned, with a child's eyes looking upwards, adults represented ugliness. Could it be that he was projecting his romantic and democratic socialist vision of how his beloved working classes looked upon the fat-cat capitalists cunningly denuding them of all the dignities and comforts of a decent life? Orwell's homily on what children really think of teachers over the age of thirty is not something to take with you into the classroom if you have decided teaching is to be your vocation until retirement:

> All who have passed the age of thirty are joyless grotesques, endlessly fussing about things of no importance and staying alive without, as far as the child can see, having anything to live for. Only child life is real life. The schoolmaster who imagines that he is loved and trusted by his boys is, in fact, mimicked and laughed at behind his back. An adult who does not seem dangerous nearly always seems ridiculous (Davison 1998: 384).

The Goldsmiths conference generated a rich range of presentations and papers about Orwell teaching as well as teaching Orwell. Orwell's critical challenging of the distortions and falsifying of media communication makes him one of the founding theorists of media and cultural studies. He recognised the direct links between education and media literacy; particularly the content of popular culture from boys' weeklies to national newspapers. Professor Tim Luckhurst and Lesley Phippen's paper offers new research and understanding of the struggle Orwell had in combatting what he saw as a failure of public understanding of a key wartime policy. German civilians were being deliberately targeted in RAF carpet bombing of German cities. Orwell pitched his political writing in *Tribune* in direct opposition to the influential pacifist and author of *Testament of Youth* (1933), Vera Brittain. Luckhurst and Phippen explore why this acute debate on the justice of war and its methodology had no traction in mainstream newspapers and the BBC. And why and how would Vera Brittain deliberately misrepresent Orwell's position after his death in 1950.

Next, Henk Vynckier (who did not attend the conference but presents a highly original paper on its overall theme) provides the clearest indication of the resonance of Orwell's writing across cultures, languages, human societies and, indeed, technological platforms. Professor Vynckier originated the first paperless literature course (with mixed results) in his university in Taiwan. As Vynckier says, Orwell, of all modern authors, appeared rather apt to be the focus of a new academic module dependent on a delivery by new technologies and the internet. There was something curiously ironic about his literature being taught in this way when he had so presciently predicted the widespread introduction of technologies of surveillance and related visual technologies.

This author's paper investigates the significance of Orwell's adventures in education. How credible were his views on teaching and the nature of the education that he received? How good a teacher was he in the context of the professionalisation of teaching at the training colleges of the time? To what extent was his writing on education tantamount to another development of his self-fashioning and transformation from Eric Arthur Blair, child of imperialism, to the democratic socialist writer George Orwell?

Jon Preston contributes a fascinating article on how Orwell's voice lives on through the teaching of his literature among his students at the state-funded BRIT School in Croydon. The ethos of the education there is the exact opposite of what Orwell railed against. Through performance poetry and engaged study of Orwell's *Animal Farm*, Dr Preston explains how his teaching empowers socially diverse students and encourages them to develop their own voice through the arts. It is about giving the children and young people the control and their own arena for voice.

The science fiction novelist and playwright Philip Palmer next offers an article enlightening us on how the rhetoric of *Nineteen Eighty-Four* is a route to appreciating the craft of Orwell as a visionary who is able to attack lies through a 'plain' prose that rings true in every phrase. Indeed, Orwell was master of his own brand of rhetoric – Orwellian rhetoric.

Finally, Professor Sean Cubitt, in 'A Short History of Hate', explores how Orwell's fictional representation of two minutes of hate in *Nineteen Eighty-Four* has metastasised across new and social media platforms. Electronic media production of Orwell's seminal novel appears to have identified the evolution and morphing of hate communication from individual performance in community assemblies and mass rallies to an aggregation of behaviours in Twitter storms and social media bullying.

REFERENCES

Davison, Peter (ed.) (1998) *The Complete Works of George Orwell, Volume 19, It is What I Think 1947-1948*, London: Secker & Warburg

Meyers, Jeffrey (2001) *Orwell: Wintry Conscience of a Generation*, London: W. W. Norton & Company

PAPER

George Orwell Versus Vera Brittain: Obliteration Bombing and the Tolerance in Wartime of Dissent in Weekly Political Publications

TIM LUCKHURST AND LESLEY PHIPPEN

In the summer of 1944, George Orwell used his column in Tribune *to launch a ferocious assault on arguments advanced by the peace campaigner Vera Brittain in her pamphlet* Seed of Chaos, *published that year by the Bombing Restriction Committee. By doing so, Orwell raised publicly a topic the wartime coalition sought anxiously to conceal from the public – the deliberate killing of German civilians in RAF bombardment of German cities – and he took advantage of the government's preparedness to tolerate controversy in weekly political publications which it worked carefully to exclude from mass market newspapers and BBC broadcasts. The controversy serves as an excellent example of the way in which weekly political publications were used to burnish Britain's democratic credentials in wartime. It also annoyed Vera Brittain so greatly that she would lie about it after Orwell died.*

Keywords: George Orwell, Vera Brittain, area bombing, newspapers, Second World War

INTRODUCTION

Historians have explored extensively the influence and significance of the BBC's broadcast journalism during the Second World War (see, *inter alia*, Calder 1969, 1991, Chignell 2011, Curran and Seaton 2010, McLaine 1979, Nicholas 1996). Newspaper journalism of the era has received relatively scant attention. Bingham (2009: 6) notes: 'Many generalisations have been made about newspapers, but there has been far too little detailed investigation of their contents.' This is regrettable because newspapers mattered greatly in wartime; Britons were, in Angus Calder's words (2008: 504), the world's 'most avid newspaper-readers'. Bingham (2009: 16) shows that, by the outbreak of war in 1939, consumption of national daily newspapers 'had extended beyond the lower-middle classes and become a normal feature of working class life'. Beers (2010: 13-21) puts flesh on the bones of that assertion, demonstrating that, by 1939, 80 per cent of British families read one of the popular London daily titles, the *Daily Mail*, *Daily Mirror*, *Daily Express*, *News Chronicle* and *Daily Herald*. Two thirds of middle-class families shared this habit – though many also bought a serious title such as *The Times*, *Telegraph*, *Manchester Guardian*, *Scotsman* or *Yorkshire Post*. Sunday newspapers were also immensely popular. Mass Observation's *Report on the Press*, published early in 1940, looked at the contents of newspapers, who read them and what people thought of them. One of its main conclusions was that 'Almost everybody reads newspapers, whether regularly or irregularly, thoroughly or cursorily' (Mass Observation Archive 1940).

THE POPULAR PRESS

Plainly, newspapers were selling in large numbers in 1940[1] and their sales would continue growing during the war. Equally plainly, each of the mainstream titles had a political stance and a desire to guide their readers' impressions of political events and issues. In the mass circulation press much of this steering took readers in one direction: towards belief in it as a people's war and confidence in the central theme that Britons were 'All in it Together'. This myth of equality under bombardment by the Luftwaffe, rationing, conscription and wartime bureaucracy produced some spectacular examples of newspaper propaganda. Examples not of enforced censorship, but of the much more effective version whereby editors did what the Ministry of Information wanted them to do – not because they were obliged to, but because they sincerely believed that they were acting in the national interest.

Among our absolute favourites is a story from the *Daily Mirror* (1940a) of Wednesday, 18 September 1940. Headlined 'Women Say "Let Us Shop"', this tremendous piece of keep-calm-and-carry-on propaganda during an intense part of the Blitz asserts: 'Women's chief grouse about air raids is not about the bombs. They are complaining that it is impossible to get shopping done while raids are in progress.' It quotes one 'woman shopper's' objection: 'It seems all wrong to me that trade should stop dead like that when a warning sounds.'

Another, published a week earlier (*Daily Mirror* 1940b), depicts an attractive nurse carrying a beautiful baby girl. The headline reads: 'Goering's military objectives.' A sub-head in block capitals below the first paragraph refers to the baby: 'Raids make her laugh,' it declares and the story goes on to explain: 'There was not a whimper from any one of the forty-six little patients when a children's hospital in Central London was struck by a blitzkrieg bomb on Monday night.' It is not entirely clear how the absence of a whimper can be reconciled with the report of a laugh, but the beautiful baby's behaviour offers some help. The *Mirror* explains: 'Flames spurted from the wreckage, clouds of smoke rolled down the stairs, but not so much as a frown came from Sandra.' Plainly this was a heroic example of Blitz Spirit in a child too young to be conscious of its existence. A third example deals with the astonishing fortitude under bombardment of disabled children. In October 1940, beneath the headline: 'My! Isn't this just like a picnic...', the *Daily Mirror* (1940c) explained: 'Peter Pan thought that danger was an awfully big adventure ... and that's what these brave little crippled children of the Heritage Craft Schools, Challey, Sussex, think too.' According to the reporter, it was 'fun to sit cosily in your air raid shelter eating a picnic dinner, while the Luftwaffe marauds overhead and a barrage of anti-aircraft batteries shakes the roof...'.

George Orwell was properly sceptical about the accuracy and authenticity of such reporting. McLaine (1979: 93) notes that he believed newspapers conformed too readily to the wishes of the wartime coalition. Orwell (1944a) would explain his position relatively late in the war in his 'As I Please' column for *Tribune*. Here he noted that the Ministry of Information achieved the suppression of 'undesirable or premature' news and opinion by what McLaine (1979: 3) summarises as 'participation in a conspiracy of the governing classes which had always succeeded in preventing public discussion of anything thought to be uncongenial'. Orwell was certainly clear that the problem existed and that it was not restricted to periods of national emergency:

> It is not only in wartime that the British press observes this voluntary reticence. One of the most extraordinary things about England is that there is almost no official censorship, and yet nothing that is actually offensive to the governing class gets into print, at least in any place where large numbers of people are likely to read it. If it is 'not done' to mention something or other, it just doesn't get mentioned. ... No bribes, no threats, no penalties – just a nod and a wink and the thing is done. A well-known example was the business of the Abdication. Weeks before the scandal officially broke, tens or hundreds of thousands of people had heard all about Mrs Simpson and yet not a word got into the press, not even into the *Daily Worker*, although the American and European papers were having the time of their lives with the story. Yet I believe there was no definite official ban: just an official 'request' and a general agreement that to break the news prematurely 'would not do'. And I can think of other instances of good news stories failing to see the light although there would have been no penalty for printing them.

In April 1944, Orwell (1944b) wrote damningly about 'the pre-war silliness' of newspapers. He identified the *Daily Sketch* as the silliest and ranked the *Daily Mirror* second, noting that in wartime, the newspapers …

> … have not got back their prestige – on the contrary they have steadily lost prestige against the wireless – partly because they have not yet lived down their pre-war frolics, but partly also because all but a few of them retain their 'stunt' make-up. … The belief that what 'is in the papers' must be true has been evaporating since Northcliffe set out to vulgarise journalism, and the war has not yet arrested the process.

A fortnight later he revisited the topic of newspapers, describing the BBC as a 'relatively sound source of news' and lamenting that popular titles 'have continued to publish without any query as to their truthfulness the American claims to have sunk the entire Japanese fleet several times over' (Orwell 1944c). He was right about the mass circulation press. However, his comment about places 'where large numbers of people are likely to read it' omits any explanation of the role played by weekly political publications to which the authorities consciously turned a blind eye. This is additionally interesting because he wrote for one and used it as a pulpit from which to address issues of controversy that rarely troubled the pages of the national dailies.

THE ROLE OF LOW CIRCULATION WEEKLY POLITICAL PUBLICATIONS

Mass circulation newspapers did on occasion speak truth to power during the Second World War. They did so on topics including air-raid precautions, rationing and the government's reluctance to open a second front following the German invasion of the Soviet Union. In doing so they showed that questioning power in a democracy at war could demonstrate that representative democracy was worth fighting to defend. However, such dissent was unusual and it aroused fury in the war cabinet. McLaine (1979: 243) shows that Churchill 'retained an acute sensitivity to newspaper criticism'. His Labour colleagues in the coalition could be equally thin-skinned, particularly about criticism in the immensely popular *Daily Mirror*, home to wartime Britain's favourite fantasy woman, 'Jane', the gorgeous, nearly naked but always virtuous star of the title's most successful strip cartoon. As Calder (2008: 288) shows, the home secretary, Herbert Morrison, and his colleague Ernest Bevin, minister of labour, were incensed by the *Mirror's* publication in March 1942 of Philip Zec's cartoon depicting a merchant seaman adrift on a raft following a German submarine attack.[2] However, while such challenging writing and reporting in daily newspapers provoked combative responses, including threats from ministers, they tolerated dissent when it appeared in low circulation weekly political publications aimed at intelligent opinion.

TIM LUCKHURST

LESLEY PHIPPEN

Close reading of wartime editions of *Tribune*, the *New Statesman and Nation*, the *Spectator* and the *Economist* suggests that such titles were permitted to question orthodoxy and challenge policy more openly than the daily titles. These publications were read by a span of intelligent opinion that stretched from the left of the Parliamentary Labour Party to the right of the Conservative Party. Readers included MPs, ministers, senior civil servants, diplomats, lawyers, trade unionists, churchmen and leading industrialists. And the war cabinet did more than turn a blind eye to criticism circulated amongst such groups. When distributed to 'local intellectual leaders …, teachers, professional men' (Hyams 1963: 242), they functioned as a useful safety valve. The conspiracy of the governing classes that kept unpalatable news and opinions out of the mass circulation titles plainly – and, on occasion, explicitly – regarded sporadic demonstrations of intelligent dissent as a valuable way of burnishing Britain's democratic credentials. These credentials were particularly valuable when working to influence American opinion – a crucial aim throughout Churchill's wartime premiership. Indeed, when Kingsley Martin, editor of the *New Statesman*, visited America in 1942, he was invited to the White House for an exclusive audience with the President and Mrs Roosevelt (ibid: 234). And we should not underestimate the impact of these concessions. As Schudson (2008: 15) demonstrates, the power of newspapers cannot be assessed by their circulation alone: 'How many readers may not matter as much as which readers they are and how intensely and instrumentally they read.'

And readers of the intelligent wartime weeklies had cause to read closely. These titles were able to dedicate space which national newspapers could not spare to discussion of moral and strategic arguments. Wartime paper rationing affected them too but, while the dailies felt obliged to squeeze as much news as possible into their reduced editions, the weeklies could leave such reporting to the BBC and Fleet Street dailies. They pursued intelligent debate with creativity and passion, and none more enthusiastically than *Tribune*, the weekly newspaper founded in 1937 by two wealthy Labour MPs from the party's socialist left, Sir Stafford Cripps and George Strauss. Hamstrung in the first year of war by its allegiance to Stalin's *diktat* that this was an imperialist war in which the duty of the proletariat was to pursue a policy of revolutionary defeatism, *Tribune* abandoned Stalinism in 1940 following the Soviet Union's invasion of Finland (Jones 1977: 48-9). In 1941 Aneurin Bevan MP, one of the leaders of the pro-war Labour left in the Parliamentary Labour Party, was appointed editor. Together with Jon Kimche, a historian and journalist, Bevan directed *Tribune's* editorial policy between 1941 and 1945.[3]

The new editorial team's enthusiasm for controversy was, in the words of a 1941 *Tribune* promotional slogan: 'Fresh and Fearless'

(*Tribune* 1941). Bevan frequently used his own wartime columns in the title to criticise ministers and policy. But, as George Orwell prepared to join the title as literary editor in the autumn of 1943, *Tribune* relished the recruitment of a truly expert controversialist. An early September issue, No. 350 (*Tribune* 1943a), advertised its pride and excitement about Orwell's involvement. It sported a bright pink glossy band stapled to the cover,[4] declaring: 'CONTRIBUTIONS BY J. B. PRIESTLEY, GEORGE ORWELL, ETHEL MANNIN, RHYS DAVIES.' The colour alone was a rare and cheering contrast to drab wartime monotony. An editorial alerting readers to the formal recruitment of 'the well-known writer and critic' appeared in late November (*Tribune* 1943c). Orwell relished the opportunity too and his 'As I Please' columns for *Tribune* have been the subject of scholarly attention. Paul Anderson's (2006) edited collection, 'Orwell in *Tribune*', is particularly helpful. But one argument in which Orwell engaged as a *Tribune* columnist has received less attention than it deserves. This is surprising because it advertised a controversy the government was determined to disguise and illustrates admirably the extent to which dissenting opinion in a title such as *Tribune* was tolerated, despite the threat it posed to government policy and even to relations with a crucial ally.

THE MORALITY AND PRACTICALITY OF AREA BOMBING

The subject Orwell chose was the purpose, morality and effectiveness of the RAF's area bombing of German cities. *Tribune* took an interesting line on this topic. While its fellow left-of-centre weekly, the *New Statesman and Nation*, confirmed its reputation for moral hand-wringing, giving substantial backing to George Bell, Bishop of Chichester, and the small group of Labour MPs who joined him in the Bombing Restriction Committee,[5] *Tribune* criticised area bombing as inefficient and wasteful of RAF lives. Thus, in an editorial comment published just before Orwell joined the staff, it explained: 'Casualties in German cities have been about twenty times greater than all the British casualties in air raids here. … The sufferers in these raids are not, of course, the Nazis but, to a large extent, the Nazi war machine and, to a new and greater extent, the civilian population' (*Tribune* 1943b). *Tribune* was not persuaded that such bombing could end the war. It argued that only the defeat of the Nazi land armies could do that. It believed the RAF should be diverted from area raids to attacks intended to support Allied troops. Just weeks later in early 1944, very shortly after Orwell joined *Tribune*, Vera Brittain, the eloquent feminist and pacifist who had served as a Voluntary Aid Detachment nurse during the First World War, published *Seed of Chaos* (1944a), a pungent denunciation of the Allied policy of destroying German industrial cities in massive round-the-clock raids. Reprinted in the United States as *Massacre by Bombing* (Brittain 1944b: 49-64), her eloquent polemic offered eye-witness accounts of the consequences of RAF raids extracted from neutral Swiss and Swedish newspaper reports and from German sources. One extract from the Stockholm newspaper, *Aftonbladet*, quoted a Danish consular official who had survived the ferocious bombardment of Hamburg in the final week of July 1943: 'Hamburg has ceased to exist. I can only tell what I saw with my own eyes – district after district razed to the ground. When you drive through Hamburg you drive through corpses. They are all over the streets and even in the tree-tops' (Brittain 1944b: 58). Another, from the Swiss *St Gallen Tagblatt* described the aftermath of devastating raids on Berlin: 'It was nerve shattering to see women, demented after the raids, crying continuously for their lost children, or wandering speechless through the streets with dead babies in their arms' (Brittain 1944b: 55).

Vera Brittain (1944b: 50) argued that the saturation bombing of cities such as Cologne, Hamburg and Berlin – and the fire storms that often ensued as the RAF became expert in combined high explosive and incendiary attacks – meant Britain was inflicting upon innocent German civilians 'agonising forms of death and injury comparable to the worst tortures of the Middle Ages'. She warned that the action by RAF Bomber Command 'morally damages the soul of a nation' (1944b: 51) and detected 'irrefutable evidence of the moral and spiritual abyss into which we have descended' (1944b: 57). She quoted extensively from an account of the consequences of firestorm in Hamburg written by the editor of the *Baseler Nachrichten* (*Basle News*). He described tens of thousands of German civilians in bomb shelters being 'suffocated, charred and reduced to ashes' (Brittain 1944b: 53). Contemplating British newspaper reports of an RAF raid on Remscheid on the night of 30-31 July 1943, Brittain conjured her own vision of 'frantic children pinned beneath the burning wreckage, screaming to their trapped mothers for help as the uncontrollable fires come nearer' (1944b: 60). She was appalled by a Swiss correspondent's account for *Das Volksrecht* of an RAF raid on Wuppertal during which, 'Numerous victims ran around aimlessly like burning torches until they died' (1944b: 61). For Brittain, area bombing invited vicious reprisal attacks and caused 'moral deterioration which displays itself in a loss of sensitivity and callous indifference to suffering' (1944b: 62).

Vera Brittain's stance attracted support and respect in the *New Statesman,* the *Guardian* and the *Spectator*. *Tribune* made little effort to lament German suffering. It preferred to praise the courage and expertise of RAF air crews and to challenge the practical value of area bombing. It was conscious that 'air bombardment has become a terrible weapon – far worse than anything experienced in this country, and there is no doubt widespread and silent gratitude to the RAF and the Red Army for having saved this island greater ordeal' (*Tribune* 1943d). But the policy promoted a 'dangerous fallacy'. Air Marshall Arthur Harris's colossal, four-engine heavy bombers were 'ill-suited to tactical work with land forces' which might hasten the end of the war – hence they had to be used for bombing cities (*Tribune* 1944a). This, *Tribune* insisted, would not hasten the war's end. Indeed, it appeared to be provoking the same stubborn resistance that German bombing of British cities had caused.

George Orwell's review of *Seed of Chaos* appeared in May 1944. He acknowledged it as 'an eloquent attack on indiscriminate or "obliteration" bombing', before advising readers that:

> No one in his senses regards bombing, or any other operation of war, with anything but disgust. On the other hand, no decent person cares tuppence for the opinion of posterity. And there is something very distasteful in accepting war as an instrument and at the same time wanting to dodge responsibility for its more obviously barbarous features. Pacifism is a tenable position, provided you are willing to take the consequences, but all talk of limiting or humanising war is sheer humbug. ... Why is it worse to kill civilians than soldiers? Heaven knows how many people our blitz on Germany has killed and will kill, but you can be quite certain it will never come anywhere near the slaughter that has happened on the Russian front (Orwell 1944d).

Tribune readers immediately made it plain that they were not united in support for their columnist. Several wrote to contest what they considered to be his relativism and aggression. In July, the literary editor came out fighting: 'It was the fascist states who started this practice,' he reminded them, 'and as long as the air war went in their favour they avowed their aims quite clearly.' Warming to his theme, he insisted on 'dealing with' the 'parrot cry' against 'killing women and children'. For Orwell:

> It is probably somewhat better to kill a cross section of the population than to kill only the young men. If the figures published by the Germans are true and we have really killed 1,200,000 civilians in our raids, that loss of life has probably harmed the German race somewhat less than a corresponding loss on the Russian front or in Africa and Italy (1944e).

Those who opposed the killing of German women were guilty of 'sheer sentimentality' and Orwell thought child casualties were probably exaggerated. 'Contrary to what some of my correspondents seem to think, I have no enthusiasm for air raids, either ours or the enemy's', but he believed that 'objections to the use of force in a total war are utterly hypocritical' (1944f). Readers' letters objecting strenuously to his stance continued to arrive. So, in early August, Orwell returned to the topic of saturation bombing, noting that:

A correspondent who disagreed with me very strongly added that he was by no means a pacifist. He recognised, he said, that 'the Hun had got to be beaten'. He merely objected to the barbarous methods that we are now using. Now, it seems to me that you do less harm by dropping bombs on people than by calling them 'Huns'. Obviously, one does not want to inflict death and wounds if it can be avoided, but I cannot feel that mere killing is all-important. We shall all be dead in less than a hundred years, and most of us by the sordid horror known as 'natural death' (1944g).

Walzer (1971: 17-18) reminds us that Orwell even asserted a moral case for killing German civilians: 'Bombing, suggested Orwell, ... brought the true character of modern warfare home to the civilian population, to all those people who supported the war, even enjoyed it, only because they did not feel its effects; now they felt them and so war was less likely in the future.' Though, the philosopher notes: 'I doubt there is enough evidence for this argument to actually lead anybody to begin bombing cities; it is an apology after the fact, and not a very convincing one.'

CONFRONTING GOVERNMENT POLICY

His criticism of Vera Brittain is not atypical Orwell. His case is blunt, uncompromising and occasionally dismissive. He recognises the sheer nastiness of area bombing. He harbours no delusions that it is aimed at exclusively military targets. He knows civilians are dying in colossal numbers and that this is entirely deliberate. He is only wrong about the child casualties. They were not exaggerated. Deep shelters offered no protection against fire storm. But his stance put him directly at odds with government policy – which was to pretend that civilian lives were, to use a modern term, collateral damage in raids carefully planned to hit industrial and military infrastructure. Indeed, the argument with which Orwell defended area bombing challenged British government policy as directly as Vera Brittain's moral fury did. Why? Because it recognised that area bombing caused mass civilian casualties and, crucially, that it intended to do so. This the government had worked very hard to disguise. Middlebrook (1980: 343-344) describes the British government's official utterings about area bombing between 1942 and 1945 as:

> ... a three-year period of deceit on the British public and world opinion. It was felt to be necessary that the exact nature of RAF bombing should not be revealed. ... The deceit lay in the concealment of the fact that the areas being most heavily bombed were nearly always city centres or densely populated residential areas, which rarely contained any industry.

It was this deceit that Orwell confronted and exposed, not in a pamphlet for a much disparaged, fringe campaign group, the Bombing Restriction Committee, but in a national weekly newspaper freely available throughout the United Kingdom and widely read by opinion formers.

Air Marshall Sir Arthur 'Bomber' Harris's strategy saw RAF Bomber Command launch thousand-bomber raids against cities including Cologne, Essen, Bremen and Hamburg. Harris pleaded with the Prime Minister and his air minister, Sir Archibald Sinclair, to acknowledge plainly that these attacks involved the deliberate murder of civilians. In October 1943, he wrote to Sinclair demanding that the tactics pursued by British and American bombers be 'unambiguously and publicly stated. That aim is the destruction of German cities, the killing of German workers and the disruption of civilised community life throughout Germany'. Harris asked, in particular, that the air minister tell the British public that the killing of German civilians by RAF Lancaster bombers was not a 'by-product of attempts to hit factories'. Rather, such slaughter was among the 'accepted and intended aims of our bombing policy' (TNA 1943).

Plainly, Harris took a view almost indistinguishable from the one Orwell articulated in his critique of Vera Brittain. The Air Marshall knew that true precision bombing was beyond the competence of RAF heavy bombers and their brave, vulnerable crews. He developed his policy of area bombing specifically to kill and de-house German workers. Choosing to identify any enemy civilian engaged in economic activity as a contributor to the Nazi war effort, he ensured the RAF heavies always attacked either city centres or densely populated residential areas. Harris knew this meant the deliberate and systematic killing of women, children and old men. Ministers knew it too, but they were determined to disguise the brutal truth. They used a series of euphemisms to describe area bombing raids. Grayling (2006: 183) recalls that these included 'blanketing an industrial district', 'neutralising the target' and 'softening up an area'. Connelly (2002:42) has demonstrated that: 'The government was extremely worried about this aspect of the war, fearing that the strategy gave the Germans a propaganda weapon that might affect Britain's position as the power occupying the "moral high ground" in the conflict.' And disguising the brutal reality was not only intended to shield ministers from domestic controversy. It was also necessary to avoid tension with Britain's American ally.

Bomber Command knew that the USAAF's policy of bombing in daylight was producing casualty rates among air crew even more catastrophic than those endured by RAF crews on night-time missions. But the Americans maintained the fiction that their daylight raids allowed them to conduct real precision bombing. In all their public rhetoric, the commanders of the United States Strategic Air Forces in Europe remained stubbornly committed to the pretence that American bomber crews were not simply aiming at military targets, they were hitting them. In fact, as Biddle (2004: 243) demonstrates, in combat conditions US Eight Air Force crews attacking Germany during the winter of 1944-45 dropped 42 per cent of their bombs more than five miles off-target. Even for those projectiles that fell within the five-mile radius, the average circular error was 2.48 miles. Nevertheless, the American public was led to believe that no American boys were engaged in murdering German civilians. To admit that the RAF was doing so deliberately and to devastating effect would have undermined the message – and British ministers were determined not to do that. Until the end of the war, Archibald Sinclair stuck to the official line. He did so even after Howard Cowan, an Associated Press war correspondent based at the Supreme Headquarters of the Allied Expeditionary Force in Europe, reported that the allies were now engaged in deliberate 'terror bombing'. Cowan's report appeared following the Dresden raids of February 1945 (*Sunday Star* 1945). Biddle (2006: 112) explains that the American military was seriously embarrassed, but Sinclair maintained the pretence that every target attacked by RAF bombers was a target of military importance and that any civilian deaths they might cause were regrettable (*Hansard* 1945).

So, by defending area bombing on the grounds that killing civilians in a total war was entirely sensible, George Orwell was playing with fire. It helped that *Tribune* itself regarded area bombing as an expensive distraction from the duty to fight an effective ground campaign. But this was Orwell at his best: determined to confront consensus and utterly contemptuous of moral relativism. We disagree with him. We think the killing of German women and children probably encouraged German soldiers to fight on when victory was no longer possible and unconditional surrender their only option (Luckhurst 2015). But we respect Orwell's instinct. Consensus is the enemy of justice. It narrows the frame of debate and conceals plausible alternatives to current orthodoxy. Orwell's wartime work for *Tribune* reveals that he often played this crucial role of challenging the dominant consensus.

His arguments against Vera Brittain and in support of area bombing offer an excellent and often overlooked case study. And Brittain certainly considered them significant. Westwood (2011) has shown that, in her autobiography (Brittain 1957), written after Orwell's death in 1950, Brittain would concoct a narrative to suggest that Orwell had reversed his opinion of area bombing and that he had reached the conclusion that she was right. Westwood argues persuasively that Brittain 'decided to quote selectively' from an article Orwell (1945) wrote from Germany for the *Observer* in April 1945 'in order to "win" her argument with Orwell in retrospect and when he could not respond'.

BRITTAIN'S LIES AND THEIR SIGNIFICANCE

Richard Westwood (2011) demonstrates clearly that Vera Brittain deliberately misrepresented Orwell in a manner that her contemporaries would have found very hard to detect, quoting selectively from his work and omitting words and phrases to distort his meaning. He notes that her mendacity allowed her to imply that, 'On the "moral touchstone" question of the bombing of civilians she … had been right and the great George Orwell wrong'. He further notes that Brittain's distortion has been amplified by her biographers, Berry and Bostridge (2008). They repeated, simplified and strengthened it by writing: 'Orwell would undergo something of a change of heart after visiting Germany as a war correspondent…' (Westwood 2011). Westwood also argues that A. C. Grayling compounded the offence by choosing 'to rely on the Berry and Bostridge book's account' when compiling his *Among the Dead Cities* (2006), his critical study of the Allied bombing of civilians. Westwood's detective work is laudable, and the misrepresentation of Orwell is more than a literary offence. It risks diluting the significance of a fine example of dissenting wartime journalism which demonstrates exactly why intelligent publications such as *Tribune* played an important part in upholding Britain's democratic tradition.

CONCLUSION

Connelly shows that German bombing of Britain spawned popular demand for harsh revenge and that this was vividly expressed in popular titles; the *Daily Mirror* would demand a 'gloves off' policy and describe the area bombing of Berlin as: 'The only effective method available to us in self-defence' (Connelly 2002: 47). This leading popular left-wing title treated critics of area bombing with contempt, insisting: 'The air war is no time for lecturers and gloved persons wishing to live up to a high standard of ancient chivalry' (Connelly 2002: 48). On the right, the *Daily Express* and *Daily Mail* were equally pugnacious. Knapp (2013: 51) argues that British newspapers did not celebrate the agonies of German civilians but notes that 'triumphalism over the scale of the bombing was routine'. But this mass market journalism did not address, still less concede, the central truth that RAF Bomber Command set out to kill civilians as a conscious act of policy.

NOTES

[1] Illustrative newspaper circulation figures are available in the last complete pre-war survey by the Audit Bureau of Circulations (ABC) completed in 1939. These show that the largest selling popular title, the *Daily Express*, had a daily circulation of 2,510,019 copies. Its Conservative rival, the *Daily Mail*, trailed behind with approximately 1,500,000 daily sales. On the left, the *Daily Mirror* sold approximately 2,500,000 copies (according to figures compiled by its proprietors) and the ABC survey shows the Liberal *News Chronicle* sold 1,298,757. Precise figures for the *Daily Herald* are not available, but ABC figures show that it achieved a daily sale of 2,113,856 copies in the first post-war survey compiled in 1948

TIM LUCKHURST

LESLEY PHIPPEN

[2] Zec's drawing was accompanied by a caption declaring: 'The Price of Petrol Has Been Increased by One Penny – Official.' It was intended to remind readers that they should not complain too much about rationing and rising prices. Morrison and Bevin interpreted it as a criticism of government for allowing sailors to suffer in the interests of profiteers. Calder (2008: 288) offers a complete account of the controversy which included threats to suspend publication of the newspaper

[3] Bevan was officially editor, but lacked the technical skill and time required to perform the role full time. This Kimche did

[4] In September 2016, I (Tim Luckhurst) was able to inspect a pristine copy of this shiny band in the Cambridge University Library which keeps a complete run of wartime editions of *Tribune*. It is the only example of such promotion I have found in a wartime edition of *Tribune*

[5] The Bombing Restriction Committee was formed in May 1942 by a group including Bishop George Bell, Corder Catchpool, a First World War conscientious objector and member of the Peace Pledge Union, non-pacifist Professor Stanley Jevons and others. It called on the British government to cease bombing German civilians and to target only military sites

REFERENCES

Anderson, Paul (ed.) (2006) *Orwell in Tribune: 'As I Please' and Other Writings 1943-1947*, London: Politico's

Beers, Laura (2010) *Your Britain: Media and the Making of the Labour Party*, Cambridge, MA and London: Harvard University Press

Berry, Paul and Bostridge, Mark (2008) *Vera Brittain: A Life*, London: Virago

Biddle, Tammy Davis (2004) *Rhetoric and Reality in Air Warfare*, Princeton and Oxford: Princeton University Press

Biddle, Tammy Davis (2006) Wartime Reactions, Addison, Paul and Crang, Jeremy (eds) *Firestorm: The Bombing of Dresden 1945*, London: Pimlico pp 96-122

Bingham, Adrian (2009) *Family Newspapers? Sex, Private Life and the British Popular Press 1918-1978*, Oxford: Oxford University Press

Brittain, Vera (1944a) *Seed of Chaos: What Mass Bombing Really Means*, London: Bombing Restriction Committee

Brittain, Vera (1944b) Massacre by bombing: The facts behind the British-American attack on Germany, *Fellowship*, Vol. X, No. 3

Brittain, Vera (1957) *Testament of Experience*, London: Gollancz

Calder, Angus (1969) *The People's War: Britain 1939-1945*, London: Jonathan Cape

Calder, Angus (1991) *The Myth of the Blitz*, London: Jonathan Cape

Calder, Angus (2008) *The People's War*, London: Pimlico, twelfth edition

Chignell, Hugh (2011) *Public Issue Radio: Talks, News and Current Affairs in the Twentieth Century*, London: Palgrave Macmillan

Connelly, Mark (2002) The British people, the press and the strategic air campaign against Germany, 1939-45, *Contemporary British History*, Vol. 16, No. 2 pp 39-58

Curran, James and Seaton, Jean (2010) *Power Without Responsibility: Press, Broadcasting and the Internet in Britain*, Abingdon: Routledge, seventh edition

Daily Mirror (1940a) Women say 'Let us shop', Wednesday, 18 September p. 3

Daily Mirror (1940b) Goering's military objectives, Wednesday, 11 September p. 7

Daily Mirror (1940c) My! Isn't this just like a picnic…, Friday, 11 October p. 7

Foot, Michael (1962) Cited in *Spartacus Educational*. Available online at http://spartacus-educational.com/Jtribune.htm, accessed on 19 June 2017

Grayling, Anthony Clifford (2006) *Among the Dead Cities: Was the Allied Bombing of Civilians in WWII a Necessity or a Crime?*, London: Bloomsbury

House of Commons *Hansard* (1945) Col. 1847-1930, 6 March

Hyams, Edward (1963) *The New Statesman: The History of the First Fifty Years*, London: Longmans

Jones, Bill (1977) *The Russia Complex: The British Labour Party and the Soviet Union*, Manchester: Manchester University Press

Knapp, Andrew (2013) The Allied bombing offensive in the British media, Knapp, Andrew and Footitt, Hilary (eds) *Liberal Democracies at War: Conflict and Representation*, London: Bloomsbury pp 39-66

Luckhurst, Tim (2015) An unworkable policy which encourages the enemy to fight to the last gasp: The depiction in British and American newspapers of the Allied policy of unconditional surrender for Germany, 1943–1945, *Journalism Studies*, Vol. 16, No. 6 pp 887-903

McLaine, Ian (1979) *Ministry of Morale: Home Front Morale and the Ministry of Information in World War II*, London: George Allen & Unwin

Mass Observation Archive (MOA) (1940) *File Report* 126, Report on the Press

Middlebrook, Martin (1980) *The Battle of Hamburg*, London: Allen Lane

Nicholas, Sian (1996) *The Echo of War: Home Front Propaganda and the Wartime BBC, 1939-45*, Manchester: Manchester University Press

Orwell, George (1944a) *Tribune*, 'As I Please', No. 393, 7 July p. 12

Orwell, George (1944b) *Tribune*, 'As I Please', No. 380, 7 April p. 12

Orwell, George (1944c) *Tribune*, 'As I Please', No. 382, 21 April p. 12

Orwell, George (1944d) *Tribune*, 'As I Please', No. 386, 19 May p. 11

Orwell, George (1944e) *Tribune*, 'As I Please', No. 394, 14 July p. 12

Orwell, George (1944f) *Tribune*, 'As I Please', No. 394, 14 July p. 12

Orwell, George (1944g) *Tribune*, 'As I Please', No. 397, 4 August p. 11

Orwell, George (1944h) *Tribune*, 'As I Please', No. 396, 28 July pp 12-13

Orwell, George (1945) Future of a ruined Germany: Rural slum cannot help Europe, *Observer*, 8 April p. 5

Schudson, Michael (2008) *Why Democracies Need an Unlovable Press*, Cambridge: Polity

Sunday Star (1945) Terror bombing gets allied approval as step to victory, 18 February pp 1, 4

TNA: AIR (1943) 2/7852 Harris letter, 25 October

Tribune (1941) *Tribune*: Fresh and fearless, No. 223, 4 April p. 1

Tribune (1943a) Contributions By…, No. 350, 10 September, appended to p. 1

Tribune (1943b) What's happening, No. 359, 12 November p. 3

Tribune (1943c) Ourselves, No. 361, 26 November p. 5

Tribune (1943d) What's happening, No. 363, 10 December p. 3

Tribune (1944a) A dangerous fallacy, No. 367, 7 January pp 6-7

Walzer, Michael (1971) Why was this war different?, *Philosophy and Public Affairs*, No. 1 pp 3-21

Westwood, Richard (2011) Vera Brittain versus George Orwell, *orwellsocietyblog*. Available online at https://orwellsocietyblog.wordpress.com/2012/02/12/vera-brittain-versus-george-orwell-by-richard-westwood/, accessed on 15 June 2017

TIM LUCKHURST

LESLEY PHIPPEN

NOTE ON THE CONTRIBUTORS

Tim Luckhurst is Professor of Journalism at the University of Kent and founding Head of the University's Centre for Journalism. He is the author of *This is Today, A Biography of the Today Programme* (Aurum Press 2001) and *Responsibility Without Power – Lord Justice Leveson's Constitutional Dilemma* (Abramis Academic 2012). He has published work on newspaper journalism during the Second World War in journals including *Journalism Studies, Ethical Space* and *British Contemporary History*. He contributes frequently to *British Journalism Review*.

Lesley Phippen was a lecturer in law and Director of Graduate Studies in the University of Kent's Centre for Journalism until 2016. She has published in journals including *New Law Journal, British Contemporary History, Index on Censorship* and *British Journalism Review*.

PAPER

Big Brother Is Coming to an iPad Near You: Teaching Orwell in Taiwan

HENK VYNCKIER

In spring 2011, a seminar for third and fourth year university students entitled 'The Essential Orwell: An iTunes U Seminar' was taught in the Department of Foreign Languages and Literatures at Tunghai University, in Taichung, Taiwan. This 'Essential Orwell' seminar dispensed with traditional textbooks and, adopting e-texts and other online materials, became the first paperless literature course taught at Tunghai University. The present study examines the institutional dynamic which led to the development of this iTunes U Orwell course. It also surveys the various Orwell texts and related materials which the students accessed online and assesses their learning experience and interest in Orwell's writings and legacy. Throughout, this paper highlights the special relevance of Orwell, the creator of Big Brother, to contemporary discussions regarding digital technology and the internet.

Keywords: George Orwell, paperless literature classroom, online courseware, iTunes University, industry-academia cooperation, surveillance

'MODERN LIFE TAKES PLACE ON-SCREEN'

In February 2011, Big Brother came to an iPad near me. The arrival of this eminent personage, famous for being the one who is always 'watching' us, resulted from a decision I made in December 2010 to participate in a new teaching programme and offer an Orwell seminar under the title of 'The Essential Orwell: An iTunes U Course'. I had taught Orwell before in the usual manner with standard course anthologies and pocket books, but this 'Essential Orwell' seminar, which met in the spring of 2011, dispensed with printed books and, adopting e-texts and other online learning materials as the medium of instruction, became the first so-called paperless literature course taught at my university. The undertaking attracted considerable attention, and I was invited to report on my experience in a university curriculum workshop the following semester. I also taught the same seminar again two years later in 2013. Yet, looking back now some half a decade later, I conclude that, while valid pedagogical concerns inspired the creation of the new module, the decision to teach Orwell with online learning materials produced mixed results and was not as warmly embraced by students as might have been expected. Nor, as it turned out, were we able to proceed entirely without books and printed materials, and I eventually reintroduced print-titles as my primary medium of instruction. Big Brother, in other words, certainly made it to an iPad near me, but unfortunately also stumbled upon arrival.

The inspiration to take on this teaching assignment and develop a paperless Orwell seminar proceeded from a meeting of university administrators in early December 2010 when the dean of academics launched a scheme to promote iPad-based courses. The iPad, then a brand-new device, had been much in the news throughout 2010 ever since legendary Apple CEO Steve Jobs had introduced this latest 'wonder gadget' in one of his patented masterful press conferences in San Francisco on 27 January 2010. iPads only went on sale in Taiwan in the fall of 2010, however, and by that time consumer interest was such that the first shipment sold out within days.

Taiwanese consumers are generally well-informed regarding developments in IT as successive governments have invested heavily in IT infrastructure and internet access is widely available around the island in the workplace, schools, private homes, and even public spaces. Taiwan, moreover, hosts several major communication and IT manufacturers such as HTC, ASUS, ACER and BENQ, as well as contract manufacturers who assemble Apple products, including iPhones and iPads, in their offshore assembly plants in China. Taiwan's economy, therefore, is much affected by the American tech giant and so-called Apple concept stocks involving Apple contract manufacturers and suppliers impact on its stock market greatly. For all these reasons, the iPad, already a big hit with consumers in the West, was guaranteed a warm reception in IT-savvy Taiwan when it reached the island in the fall of 2010.

Another, more local aspect of the iPad story, which influenced the launch of the Orwell iTunes seminar, follows from the fact that a well-known bookstore chain had been chosen as one of the official distributors and was offering iPads at some of its campus bookstores around the island, including at the branch of a cross-town rival institution, but not at our own campus branch. Photographs of students and other customers lining up outside the store had been published in the press, generating some free publicity for our competitor. As our dean of academics, the main proponent of the teaching initiative, noted during a meeting of the university curriculum committee several days later, iPads clearly were in the news. Not only had they captured the attention of young people, but they could also be used in combination with Apple's well-stocked iTunes digital content library and affiliated iTunes University educational platform to give students access to an impressive range of learning materials.

Perhaps, then, this would be a good opportunity to experiment and start up some new teaching modules with such online learning tools. The dean further stated that, even though course offerings for the second semester had been finalised two weeks earlier, he welcomed late additions of iTunes U courses to the programme for the spring semester and promised substantial support, including iPads and funding for content downloads, for any instructors willing to develop new course modules. There were two caveats, however. Interested teachers were asked to commit themselves within forty-eight hours. In addition, there was no guarantee that iPads would be available to instructors at the start of the second semester in late February as the first shipment was already sold out and the second shipment was not expected until early March.

One other factor, which was not touched upon in the meeting but gradually came into view over the course of the next few months, was that the university was going to be audited the next fall by the Higher Education Evaluation and Accreditation Council of Taiwan (HEEACT), and a preliminary mock evaluation was scheduled for that spring. Any teaching initiatives that could still be launched at this stage to diversify the range of courses and services offered to students would surely be helpful to improve the school's standing in the eyes of the accreditation committee. This, I realised later, was one of the reasons why the iTunes modules were fast-tracked for approval and eligible for special subsidies. Considering all these factors half a decade later, it is evident that, above and beyond my own pedagogical interests, fortuitous timing and sheer administrative pluck played an important role in the launch of the teaching initiative.

In any event, when a colleague reported to me about the call for course proposals, I was intrigued. In a study published in 1999, visual culture scholar Nicolas Mirzoeff noted: 'Modern life takes place on-screen' (Mirzoeff 1999: 1). More than a decade later these words sounded more convincing than ever before, and the idea of teaching a paperless course of this nature, therefore, appealed to me. Students, I agreed, were fascinated by the new technologies and always ready to explore the latest devices and content platforms. Literature teachers, however, seemed reluctant to experiment with new media. Yet, Netbooks, Tablet PCs, eReaders, and smartphones had been eagerly welcomed by consumers as communication devices, productivity tools, entertainment systems and educational aids. Moreover, it is increasingly in an electronic format transmitted via these devices and purchased from Amazon, Barnes and Noble,

HENK VYNCKIER

Apple's iBook Store and other online platforms that literary texts and other cultural media continue to reach new generations of readers. Perhaps, then, it was also increasingly true that 'modern education takes place on-screen'.

Another consideration that came into play is that Orwell, of all modern authors, appeared pre-eminently suited to a course centred around new technologies and the internet. Few twentieth-century authors have remained more relevant to contemporary debates about society and politics than Orwell and phrases such as 'Big Brother is watching you', 'Newspeak', 'doublethink', 'Freedom is slavery', 'All animals are created equal, but some are more equal than others' etc. ... continue to be quoted daily. What is more, not only is he extensively referenced on the internet and in the mass media, but he also predicted the widespread introduction of technologies of surveillance and related visual technologies, that is, specifically the kinds of technologies I was going to use in the seminar. Orwell, namely, worked for the Eastern Service of the BBC as a talks producer from 1941 to 1943 and was aware of the experiments which were taking place at the time with a new medium called television broadcasting. Six years following his resignation from the BBC, he published his last novel *Nineteen Eighty-Four*, and in that novel so-called telescreens loom large in every home and place of work. Functioning around the clock, these two-way communication devices broadcast government propaganda and at the same time monitor citizens' every action, conversation and even facial expression. All this, of course, at the service of Big Brother, the revered leader of Oceania. Today, some sixty years following the novel's original publication, the wall-mounted telescreens of *Nineteen Eighty-Four*, ruthlessly efficient in their use as surveillance and propaganda tools, have been succeeded by a multitude of mobile devices. Indeed, Orwell's vision in *Nineteen Eighty-Four* of a telescreen in every room is now coming true in a world in which there is a pocket-sized screen of some kind in every handbag or briefcase. Clearly, Orwell's terrifying last novel refuses to die and reemerges time after time to engage us in debates about our intellectual positions and political values. Hence, my reflection: 'Big Brother is coming to an iPad near you.'[1]

Another factor which influenced my decision concerned my interest in archives, museums and material culture and previous work on Western expatriate missionaries and life writers in China and Taiwan.[2] Digital technologies were and continue to be the new frontier in this research area as library holdings and museum collections are continually being scanned or photographed. Indeed, by 2011 relevant collections of Orwell photographs, first edition scans and other materials illustrating British history and culture in the first half of the twentieth century had been uploaded to the internet and could readily be shared in class. There was little risk, in other words, of students being confronted with a hollow, ahistorical, cyber Orwell. On the contrary, technology would enable us to bridge the distance between our location and Orwell's faraway homeland, and situate the English writer more completely in his own world and times. I also considered in this respect that Orwell wrote insightful essays and book reviews on seaside postcards, boys' weeklies, Victorian adventure novels, crime fiction and other popular culture topics, and that this aspect of his legacy – that is, Orwell the popular culture observer – appeals to students in Taiwan given their love of manga, animation film, online games, young adult literature and other popular media. Such popular culture subjects, I surmised, offered endless opportunities for digging deeper into Orwell's work and engaging in online research and in-class discussions bringing together Western and Asian cultures.

I note, finally, that my department has a policy of teaching exclusively in English, which is not always the case in English/Foreign Language and Literature programmes in Taiwan as many institutions distinguish between language acquisition courses, which are taught in English, and content courses, which are taught in Chinese or a mixture of English and Chinese. At Tunghai, therefore, students are required to perform all course work, including not only reading assignments but also presentations, writing assignments and class discussion in English. This also means that development in listening, speaking, reading and writing is always a basic objective in our classrooms regardless of whether the instructor is teaching a language acquisition course or content course in literature, culture or linguistics. Orwell, given his conviction that 'good prose is like a window pane' and dedication to clarity of expression, has much to offer students from this point of view as well. For all these reasons, then, I concluded that it might be a good time to give it a try, and I notified the Office of Academic Affairs that I was willing to offer an iTunes U seminar on Orwell for English majors in the Department of Foreign Languages and Literatures. The course was added to the online course registration system within days and in due time thirteen junior and senior students registered for the seminar. A colleague in the department, meanwhile, also developed an iTunes U course for postgraduate students in our Teaching English as a Foreign Language (TEFL) MA Programme.

'THE ESSENTIAL ORWELL: AN ITUNES U COURSE'

All in all, therefore, the seminar was shaping up as an interesting educational initiative. Students were given the opportunity to familiarise themselves with Orwell's essential writings, including not only his two most famous works *Animal Farm* and *Nineteen Eighty-four*, but also earlier works of fiction such as *Burmese Days* and *Coming Up for Air*, as well as *The Road to Wigan Pier* and *Homage to Catalonia*, and essays such as 'A Hanging', 'Shooting an Elephant', 'Boys' Weeklies', 'Why I Write', 'Thoughts on the

HENK VYNCKIER

Common Toad', 'Decline of the English Murder', 'Politics and the English Language', 'Just Junk – But Who Can Resist It?' etc. ... In doing so, they examined his lasting impact on contemporary literature and current discussions regarding politics, technology, the mass media and popular culture.

In addition, an effort was made to situate Orwell within an Asian cultural context, thus creating opportunities to study his comments on Asian societies and East-West political relations, as well as pursue comparative studies on Orwell and Taiwanese or Chinese writers and public intellectuals. The well-known Taiwanese author and former university president Li Jia-tung, for example, included *Animal Farm* and *Nineteen Eighty-Four* in his *Uncle Li's Forty Favorite Books* from 2005. In this book, Uncle Li – the uncle designation is considered highly respectable in Chinese culture and indicates the author's standing as a trustworthy mentor for young readers – recommends what he considers the forty most important books on various subjects, including nature, love, politics and other subjects. The two works by Orwell are identified as key political writings and are listed as numbers 20 and 21 respectively. Students, I knew, were familiar with Uncle Li, and more work of this nature in tracing Orwell's reception in and influence on Taiwan and other East Asian societies was encouraged to foster Asia-centric approaches to this canonical English author.[3]

This latter objective, which is important in any English/Western literature class in an Asian cultural setting, was wonderfully enhanced in the spring 2011 semester by the one-day conference on 'George Orwell: Asian and Global Perspectives' which my department hosted on 21 May 2011. The rationale for this conference was that, while Orwell is not as intensely studied in the Asian academy as he is at universities in the West, he is profoundly linked to and deserving of consideration in the Asian cultural context. Not only was he born in India and served five years (1922-1927) in the Indian Imperial Police in Burma, but he often conducted himself as an 'Asia watcher' and wrote about Asian societies and global politics throughout his career as a writer and journalist. Scholars from seven foreign countries, including prominent Orwell scholars such as John Rodden from Texas and Douglas Kerr from Hong Kong, as well as representatives from the UK-based Orwell Prize and the Japanese Orwell Society, were invited and students would be able to hear their presentations and interact with the foreign guests. As I told students, 'Big Brother is coming to a conference near you!'[4]

A third course objective, finally, was for students to explore iTunes University and other online resources for studying literature and culture. The latter goal was significant in that students in English departments and departments of foreign languages and literatures in Taiwan generally enter a variety of professional fields such as education, government service, international trade and the publishing industry, and an ability to work with new productivity and educational tools, as well as online platforms, is vital for their personal and professional development. The premise of an iTunes U course is straightforward: the course content is derived from the web-based iTunes U platform and so, ideally, students should be provided with an iPad or notebook computer with the iTunes U application from day one. As noted, though, iPads were in short supply and even the course instructor's iPad did not arrive until four weeks into the semester. The question of access to the online materials was, therefore, left for the course participants to solve, and students responded pragmatically by pressing into service their own Notebook PCs. Though not as mobile as iPads or other Tablet PCs, these Notebooks provided ready access to the online resources and a full range of productivity tools.

An alternative approach, which initially appeared to offer a way out, but in the long run turned into more of a side show, soon emerged. Thanks to an Industry-Academia Cooperation agreement with Taiwanese IT manufacturer ASUS Corporation, I obtained fifteen ASUS Eee Note eReaders and made these available to the students free of charge once classes began in February. Yet, though I initially expected that these eReaders would play a major role in the seminar, they never became more than an auxiliary device for use alongside students' Notebook PCs. The eReaders had wireless connectivity and could be interfaced with PCs with Windows operating systems, but their monochrome screens, paired down web browsing application and compatibility issues limited their functionality as learning devices. Considering the introduction of more competent devices such as the iPad and Amazon's Kindle eReader, this ASUS eReader, though newly released in late 2010, was essentially outclassed as soon as it hit the market. Students, in consequence, enjoyed receiving and exploring these free gadgets, but always retained computers as their main learning platform.[5]

Learning materials accessed from the Apple ecosystem (that is, iTunes, iTunes University, and iBooks) included the following texts, podcasts, and audio recordings: *Animal Farm*, *Nineteen Eighty-Four*, a podcast with Christopher Hitchens speaking about Orwell at George Mason University; three talks about George Orwell at University College London (this included a conversation about a stage adaptation of *Burmese Days* which had just gone into production in London); a talk with Orwell biographer Jeffrey Meyers; the classic *George Orwell 1984: A Radio Dramatisation*, presented by David Niven; *Shooting an Elephant*, read by Patrick McLean; and a discussion of *Selected Essays by Orwell* at the University of Warwick. Video selections included a one-hour video lecture by John Rodden entitled 'The Politics of Literary Reputation: How Writers Become Famous' and the 1954 BBC film adaptation

HENK VYNCKIER

of *Nineteen Eighty-Four* starring Peter Cushing. We supplemented these selections with video materials from other content providers, such as, for example, YouTube, including the 1956 animated version of *Animal Farm* by Batchelor and Halas, and a 2002 broadcast of *Think Tank* in which host Ben Wattenberg discusses 'Orwell's Century' with Christopher Hitchens and John Rodden.

Moreover, as many Orwell texts are not available within the Apple ecosystem, students also obtained paper copies of *Burmese Days*, *Coming Up for Air*, *Selected Essays*, and other texts from libraries and bookstores. Here, then, was a clear indication that the paperless method could not be sustained and needed to be propped up with more traditional media. Fortunately, this was not experienced as a problem by class participants in both 2011 and 2013, as one third of the students stated that they basically preferred books over e-texts and the remaining two thirds specified that, while they were fascinated by the new technologies, they did not reject textbooks and course anthologies *per se*. Reading the primary texts is one thing, they noted, and undertaking research and doing presentations another. For the former, books were fine; for the latter, the myriad multimedia resources of the internet were indispensable. In sum, though officially defined as a 'paperless' course, the Orwell seminar, in fact, developed into more of a mixed course. Nor did it yield any clear evidence – both in its 2011 and 2013 iterations – that young people are ready to abandon printed media altogether and collectively embrace online course methodologies.

Additional complications soon developed and revealed even more fully that not all was well in our interconnected, iTuning classroom. When we first downloaded a collection of *George Orwell Works* including *Animal Farm*, *Nineteen Eighty-Four* and twelve of Orwell's most important essays from the iTunes Store for just $4.99, we were delighted to have obtained some of the key texts for the price of a cup of cappuccino. Yet, our joy soon turned to disappointment when we discovered that the iTunes *Nineteen Eighty-Four* edition did not include the novel's appendix on 'The Principles of Newspeak'. The iTunes publisher, it seemed, had simply eliminated this appendix and ends the novel in the last chapter with the image of Winston Smith in the Chestnut Tree Café finally loving Big Brother as he listens to the news of Oceania's remarkable victory on the African front. This is, of course, ironic as it echoes the controversy some sixty years earlier when the editors of the American Book of the Month Club (BOMC) had made a similar request to Orwell. Motivated by a commercial reflex to produce an easier read, they wanted to concentrate on the narrative and publish the book without the extracts from Goldstein's 'Treatise on Oligarchical Collectivism' and the Appendix on 'The Principles of Newspeak'. Orwell refused, however, and the novel was published by the BOMC as intended by its author. As noted by biographers and critics, it was a courageous decision to insist on the integrity of one's work because the BOMC contract was a particularly lucrative one and any breakdown in the negotiations could have resulted in a loss of many tens of thousands of US dollars in copyright fees.

Our own transaction involved a mere pittance of the sums Orwell had stood to lose, but we also turned down this truncated edition and demanded and obtained a refund of the $4.99 fee. It is troubling to imagine, though, that readers who are not familiar with Orwell's work may read the novel for the first time in this version and never suspect they have been handed an incomplete text. In addition, one wonders if the iTunes publishers, who produced such an unsatisfactory edition of *Nineteen Eighty-Four*, would feel at liberty to perform similar commercially driven hatchet jobs on other texts. Would they, for example, be tempted to eliminate the 'Second Epilogue on History' from Tolstoy's *War and Peace*? How about the essayistic and other non-narrative appendices, postscripts, afterwords, intertexts, conversations and diary extracts in a whole range of modern fiction from Dostoyevsky to Robert Musil, Hermann Hesse, Jean-Paul Sartre and Aldous Huxley? Would they respect those? It is ironic, in any event, to reflect that once again Orwell was relevant. 'Big Brother is coming to an iPad near you.' Big Brother, it seems, is always coming to us in one way or another and making decisions for us. In this case, the iTunes Big Brother sliced and diced a literary classic and sold it without warning consumers that what they were buying was not the authentic product.

'GOOGLE SET TO REPLACE GOVERNMENT AS BIG BROTHER'

In assessing students' learning experience, it is important to underline that, notwithstanding these setbacks, it was generally very positive. Students are interested in Orwell, whatever form he may appear in, be it a paper or paperless one, and that for a variety of reasons. For one, he worked in a wide array of genres and modes such as realistic fiction, fairy story, dystopian fiction, comic narrative, personal memoir, faction, essays, political pamphlets and newspaper columns. For another, his work leaves room for different interpretations and allows for a diverse range of research and presentation topics involving politics, intellectual history, popular culture, journalism, mass media studies, stylistics, reception studies and so forth. Among his earlier fiction and essays, *Burmese Days* and 'Shooting an Elephant' were considered particularly interesting and relevant in view of Taiwan's colonial history ranging from the Spanish and Dutch presence in 17th century Formosa to the Japanese colonial era from 1895-1945. *Coming Up for Air* was also viewed positively due to its humorous protagonist. He is fat but believes 'there's a thin man inside every fat man' (1986 [1939]: 20), and goes in search of the England of his childhood. This latter

HENK VYNCKIER

theme of nostalgia appealed to students as their homeland has prioritised rapid industrial and economic development over nature conservation and heritage preservation. Other historical topics which were emphasised include the British Raj in India and Burma, World War Two in Europe and the blitz on London, the history of socialism, English literature between the wars, and North Korea and its Big Brother Kim Jung-il. Popular culture subjects which inspired student presentations and essays include English nursery rhymes and the 'Oranges and Lemons' nursery rhyme in *Nineteen Eighty-Four*, possible links between the American 'Sugar Candy Mountain' hobo song and Moses, the tame raven in *Animal Farm*, stage adaptations of *Animal Farm* around the world, a comparative study of *Nineteen Eighty-Four* and Michael Radford's *Nineteen Eighty-Four* film adaptation, *1984*, and the Apple Macintosh 1984 commercial and other commercials inspired by Orwell.

It was clear, moreover, that today, as in the past, the popularity of Orwell's fiction in our 24/7 connected media landscape provokes uneasy questions – many of which were particularly relevant in the context of a course that depended on Tablet and Notebook PCs and internet access. As John Rodden, one of the Orwell scholars examined by students, sketched in detail in his *The Politics of Literary Reputation: The Making and Claiming of 'Saint George Orwell'*, already upon the first publication of *Nineteen Eighty-Four* in 1949, some of the amazing cultural momentum generated by the novel was due to more than just its literary excellence. It involved a complex nexus of influences, including cooptation of his work by intellectuals and politicians, well-timed radio and television adaptations and the selection of Orwell texts for use in secondary schools. (Rodden 1989) The Cold War, moreover, was reshaping the global political landscape and government agencies in what became known as the free world, including the American Central Intelligence Agency and the British Information Research Department (IRD), deftly made use of *Animal Farm* and *Nineteen Eighty-Four* as propaganda tools and invested heavily in translation, newspaper serialisation and other popularising initiatives for these novels (Rodden 2003: 45 and 212). Today, there are similar stories regarding the choices we are offered as consumers of literary and cultural products, but this time, as we experienced with our inauthentic iTunes Orwell, the manipulators can be large international corporations as well as government agencies.

Questions regarding the Orwellian nature of life in the twenty-first century were, therefore, uppermost in the minds of students and were touched upon time and again during class discussions. A range of topics, including, for example, 'Big Brother Today', 'Big Brother in Taiwan', 'Orwell and Popular Culture', 'Film and Stage Adaptations of *Animal Farm*', and 'Orwell on Post-World War Two East Asia' were suggested as possible research and presentation subject while topics involving Big Brother in contemporary society were preferred by students. In 2011, for example, two students presenting a joint report spoke at length about 'Big Brother Today' and focused on stories in *The New York Times* and other newspapers from July 2009 which described how the online retailer, Amazon, had remotely deleted some digital editions of *Animal Farm* and *Nineteen Eighty-Four* from the Kindle readers of customers who had purchased them from Amazon's eBook library. Amazon defended its actions by noting that the deleted Orwell downloads had been added to the Kindle library by a content publisher who did not hold the copyright and Amazon, therefore, had no other choice but to intervene in this manner. Most of the affected customers, however, were not impressed with this argument and expressed their dismay at the idea of someone being able to access remotely a reading device and delete texts, including the reader's personal notes and comments on those texts. Some customers also reflected on the irony of Amazon doing this with, of all books, *Nineteen Eighteen-Four*, the very novel which symbolises censorship in the modern world (Stone 2009). Course participants, meanwhile, recalling their own experience with the truncated iTunes *Nineteen Eighty-Four*, commented on the need for stronger consumer protection amidst this rapidly evolving Brave New World of e-commerce.

Two years later, in the second iteration of the Orwell iTunes course, a second pair of students reported on the same topic and spoke at length about two new examples. The first involved the announcement in January 2012 of Google's new privacy policy when the internet giant stated that, henceforth, it would track users across the entire range of its services; including Gmail, Google Docs, Google Books, Google Maps, the YouTube video service, the social networking site Google + and all the other Google services. Users who disagreed with this policy would need to access their account settings and opt out of this new policy. The implications were immediately clear to students: as soon as you log in and for as long as you are logged in, they noted, Google is watching you and compiling detailed profiles documenting your browsing habits, online purchases, restaurant and hotel reservations, travels and possibly even religious faith and political affiliations. They also quoted an Israeli news website which vividly captured the public response with an article published online on 25 January 2012. The title of the article? 'Google set to replace government as Big Brother.' For good measure, in order not to leave any confusion as to which Big Brother was meant, the article included a shot of the telescreen image of Big Brother from the opening sequence of Michael Radford's *1984* film adaptation (Kahn 2012). Reporting on another example of Orwellian discourse in the contemporary press, the students noted that large international corporations would not entirely replace governments as Big Brother. In April 2012, for example, the government of Singapore began installing police surveillance cameras that would eventually cover all ten thousand of the city's housing blocks, and Orwellian phrases were also being applied to this situation. The well-known Singaporean political satirist Mr. Brown, for example, posted a critical comment on micro-blogging site Twitter which ended with the salute: 'Welcome to Big Brother!' (*Jakarta Globe* 2012). The students, finally, observed that anyone interested in sifting through the daily global newsfeed would be able to collect an entire portfolio of such references, and agreed with the course premise that more than ever our interconnected, iTuning, smartphoning, Googling world calls for Orwellian reflection and introspection.

BIG BROTHER IN TAIWAN

The subject 'Big Bother in Taiwan' also generated some fine presentations involving the role played by American magazines such as *Time* and *Life* in the propaganda campaigns surrounding General Chiang Kai-shek. Following their defeat in the civil war in China and their evacuation to Taiwan, Chiang and the Nationalist regime ruled Taiwan with an iron hand and placed the island under martial law for more than thirty-eight years – from 20 May 1949 until 15 June 1987: the longest period of martial law in history at the time it was lifted. Chiang, though still revered today by a minority of Taiwanese who favour unification with China, is widely viewed as a dictator by younger Taiwanese, and students were intrigued to discover that he featured ten times on the cover of *Time* magazine from 1927 to 1955. These cover images include portrait sketches and paintings (the first one in black crayon from April 1927 shows a rather menacing unsmiling young Chiang, whereas the colour paintings from the 1940s and 1950s are much more flattering and show a smiling and charismatic elder Chiang), as well as photographs from the '30s and '40s. Many of the latter show the general in military uniform in different poses (for example, seated in an official pose or standing while giving a speech or riding a horse) and a couple show him either seated or standing in a domestic setting next to Madame Chiang and wearing a Chinese gentleman's long robe. The American-educated Madame Chiang (also known as Soong Mei-ling) herself also featured on *Time* and *Life* magazine covers without her husband, and T. V. Soong, Chiang's brother-in-law and Republic of China premier from 1945 to 1947, appeared on one *Time* cover.[6] Students commented that the general had been useful to the USA, first as an ally in the war against Japan and later during the Cold War, and pointed out the Big Brother implications of much of this imagery surrounding Chiang and his family. Indeed, they concluded, there had been striking similarities between the personality cult of Chiang Kai-shek in Taiwan and that of his great rival Mao Tse-tung in China. A large portrait of the general, for example, at one time presided over the Tiananmen (Heavenly Peace) Square in Peking in the same place where the now famous portrait of Mao Tse-tung has hung ever since the proclamation of the People's Republic of China in October 1949. Much of recent Chinese history, in sum, had been 'a tale of two BBs'.

This discussion of personality cults in Taiwanese history, moreover, became even more significant to students when we examined the background story of the most famous building on our own campus and, indeed, one of the most famous buildings in Taiwan, namely the Henry W. Luce Memorial Chapel. Though every student at Tunghai University is familiar with the chapel, an early work by the Pritzker Prize-winning Chinese-American architect I. M. Pei (famous for his glass pyramid at the Louvre and many other buildings around the world) and probably takes numerous photographs of this iconic building over the course of his or her studies, few probably know all the details concerning the founding of the university and the naming of the chapel. This was also true for students in the Orwell seminar who were astonished to discover that the Rev. Henry Winters Luce (1868-1941), after whom the chapel is named, was the father of Henry Robinson Luce, the publisher of *Time* magazine who promoted Chiang and his nationalist regime so fervently during the general's long political career in China and Taiwan.

The Rev. Luce, they learned, served thirty-one years in China as a Presbyterian missionary and faculty member of Cheeloo University in Jinan, while his son, Henry R. Luce, the later publishing magnate, was born in China in 1898. Moving to the USA at the age of fifteen, Henry Luce entered a preparatory school in Connecticut before enrolling at Yale, and later pursued a career in journalism. He went on to found *Time* and *Fortune* and became the most successful magazine publisher in American history, as well as a major supporter of American foreign policy objectives and a fierce Cold Warrior who used his media empire in anti-communist campaigns around the world.[7] His single-minded devotion to these causes and authoritarian methods within his organisation did not endear him to all; radical New York intellectual and Orwell admirer Dwight MacDonald, who briefly worked for him, for example, called him 'Il Luce' after Italy's 'Il Duce' Mussolini (Harris 2016: 156). Most importantly, as far as Taiwan and Tunghai University were concerned, he provided generous financial backing to the so-called United Board for Christian Higher Education in Asia, which is headquartered in New York and was the main sponsor of Tunghai University when exiled Christian educators from the now-disbanded Christian colleges in China decided to found a new Christian university in Taichung, Taiwan, in 1955. In return for Luce's patronage, the administration of Tunghai University named its new chapel after the publisher's father. Astonished to discover this linkage between the beloved architectural masterpiece at the heart of their campus and the larger story of Cold War politics, students concluded: 'Big Brother was here a long time ago.'[8]

PAPER

HENK VYNCKIER

JUST PULP FICTION – BUT WHO CAN RESIST IT?

Another discussion topic which attracted considerable interest involved the ways in which American publishers promoted Orwell's fiction in the 1950s and 1960s and produced cover art and accompanying catchphrases and headlines to sell his fiction to a mass market audience. In other words, noting how American publishers responded to Orwell's rise to fame following the publication of *Animal Farm* in 1945 and *Nineteen Eighty-Four* in 1949 by publishing his earlier fiction from the 1930s, in many cases for the first time, students examined the paratexts, that is the cover art, publisher headlines, text blurbs, and other preliminary materials in pocket book editions by the Popular Library, Avon, and Signet Books. They concluded, interestingly, that an effort was made to sell Orwell as an author of pulp fiction. The cover page of the July 1952 Popular Library edition of *Burmese Days*, for example, defines Orwell's first novel as 'A jungle tale of hate and lust' and sports an illustration in which a scantily dressed woman (Flory's Burmese mistress Ma Hla May) peeps from behind a corner and sees Flory passionately fondling and kissing a blond woman, presumably Elizabeth Lackersteen. The text blurb on the back cover further screams: 'She knew all about love!' and another paratext headline inside the book affirms: 'For sale: one woman.' As for *Coming Up for Air*, the 1950 Avon pocket book describes this comic masterpiece from 1939 as 'George Orwell's great novel of one man's temptation' and has a drawing of the middle-aged George Bowling wistfully looking at himself as a young man sitting in the grass with a blonde. The latter leans back revealing a pair of sexy legs and rests her head against Bowling's right thigh in anticipation of her lover's kiss. The young Bowling, meanwhile, has a James Dean-type of profile and slick hairdo and the entire scene seems lifted from a contemporary Hollywood film poster.

The most bewildering of all these pocketbook Orwells in students' estimation, however, was the front cover of the Signet Book *1984* from July 1950 in which a policeman resembling a beefcake from a Superman or Flash Gordon comic book emerges from a dense crowd and stares furiously at a man standing in front of a crumbling brick wall. The latter, Winston Smith one presumes, averts his eyes and stands back to back with a carefully made-up woman in a blue overall with a large Anti-Sex League button on her chest and tight red sash around her waist, ostensibly Julia, the girl from the Fiction Department. The anti-sex message of Julia's button, though, is contradicted by the very deep cleavage of her overall and the voluptuous curve of her body as she leans back against her lover and flicks her eyes to the right in anticipation of further attention from the intruding police officer. On the wall to her left, we see a poster with a pointy-eared and slick-haired Big Brother and the famous line 'Big Brother is watching you!' Curiously, the illustrator who designed this image made BB fix his eyes on a spot above

Winston and Julia, thus creating the impression that BB is looking at the viewer outside the image and once again reminding him that 'Big Brother is watching you!' In the background, finally, two massive pyramid-like structures representing various ministries tower over the entire claustrophobic scene. This one illustration by itself, students agreed, invites a detailed discussion of a whole range of critical concepts, including state surveillance and panoptic vision, the gendered or sexual gaze, and the visual narratives and design language of comic books and science fiction film.

CONCLUSION

The present study has highlighted the importance of teaching Orwell, the creator of Big Brother, in Taiwan and confirmed that students enjoy his work regardless of whether it is presented to them via traditional paper media or new paperless formats. Foremost among Orwell's fortes, students relate to his language, sense of humour, interest in popular culture and political vision, with the latter especially being valued highly in democratic Taiwan as it uneasily considers its future vis-à-vis superpower China on the other side of the Taiwan Strait. As for the medium of instruction, though it is unlikely that the paradigm shift from old media to new media will be halted, the Orwell iTunes U seminar taught at Tunghai University in 2011 and 2013 revealed that there were still major impediments to the full-scale acceptance of online learning materials in the literature classroom. The immaturity of the technology, as well as poor decision-making by content providers who sold a key text in a truncated version while completely ignoring many other Orwell writings, presented considerable challenges. In addition, students were more attached to the printed book than anticipated and generally preferred learning methodologies which creatively mixed paper materials with digital media.

Nevertheless, it is unlikely that the Brave New World of digital education will be stopped in its tracks as hardware devices achieve greater technical maturity and e-Books continue to gain wider acceptance. Already in May 2011, for example, Amazon reported that it was selling more e-books than paperback books in the USA and a little over a year later it registered a similar success for its e-book sales in the United Kingdom (Miller and Bosman 2011; Barnett 2012). Taiwan, China, and other countries in Asia will, no doubt, follow suit. In sum, I expect to see Big Brother again on an iPad near me in the years to come. Hopefully, a good complete copy of *Nineteen Eighty-four*, with its Appendix on 'The Principles of Newspeak' intact, will still be available at that time.

NOTES

[1] For recent surveys of Orwell and surveillance, see the book chapters by Marks, Peter (2015) George Orwell and the history of surveillance studies and Zollmann, Florian (2015) *Nineteen Eighty-Four* in 2014: Power, militarism, and surveillance in Western democracies, Keeble, Richard Lance (ed.) *George Orwell Now!* New York: Peter Lang

[2] See Vynckier, Henk (2007) Museifying Formosa, Hayot, Eric et al (eds) *Sinographies: Writing China*, Minneapolis, MN: University of Minnesota Press; and Vynckier, Henk and Chang, Chihyun (2012) The life-writing of Hart, Inspector-General of the Imperial Maritime Customs Service, *CLC Web: Comparative Literature and Culture*, Vol. 14, No. 5, Article 10. Available online at http://docs.lib.purdue.edu/clcweb/

[3] Te-hsing Shan discusses Orwell's reception in Taiwan in his later journal article The Reception of George Orwell in Taiwan, *Concentric: Literary and Cultural Studies*, Vol. 40, No. 1, March 2014 pp 97-125

[4] Some of the papers from this conference were published in 'Orienting Orwell: Asian and Global Perspectives on Orwell', a special issue of *Concentric: Literary and Cultural Studies*, Vynckier, Henk and Rodden, John (eds.) Vol. 40, No. 1 (March 2014)

[5] The first week of class one student posted a lengthy note entitled 'New Toys!' on Facebook stating his delight at having received an eReader and doing a fairly detailed and generally positive technical evaluation of the device. This note then generated responses from other participants in the course. At the end of the semester, I also asked students to fill out a user satisfaction questionnaire, but found the results largely inconsequential in view of the device's limitations and the manufacturer's decision to discontinue this product line

[6] The covers with General Chiang are dated 4 April 1927; 11 December 1933; 24 February 1936; 9 November 1936; 1 June 1942; 3 September 1945; 6 December 1948 and 18 April 1955. General and Madame Chiang are featured on 26 October 1931 and 3 January 1938. Madame Chiang on 1 March 1943. T. V. Soong appears on the 18 December 1944 cover. Madame Chiang is also featured on the front cover of *Life* on 30 June 1941. Haygood, Daniel (2004) analyses the *Time* covers in Saving face: An analysis of ten *Time* magazine front covers featuring Chiang Kai-shek, presented at the 2004 annual meeting of the International Communication Association in New Orleans, LA (27 May 2004). Available online at http://citation.allacademic.com/meta/pmla_apa_research_citation/1/1/3/2/9/ pages113298/p113298-1.php, accessed on 25 February 2012

[7] For Henry Luce's foreign policy agenda, see Baughman, James L. (2001 [1987]) *Henry R. Luce and the Rise of the American News Media,* Baltimore, MD: The Johns Hopkins University Press, and Herzstein, Robert E. (2005) *Henry R. Luce, Time, and the American Crusade in Asia*, Cambridge: Cambridge University Press

[8] In 2014, the Luce Chapel received a 2014 'Keeping It Modern Grant' from the Getty Foundation to fund a study of the history of the chapel and its construction, as well as prepare for further conservation efforts. See http://www.getty.edu/foundation/initiatives/current/ keeping_it_modern/ grants_awarded.html

REFERENCES

Barnett, Emma (2012) Amazon sells more e-books than print-titles in the UK, *Guardian*, 6 August. Available online at http://www.telegraph.co.uk/technology/amazon/9455149/Amazon-sells-more-e-books-than-print-titles-in-the-UK.html, accessed on 7 August 2012

Harris, Sarah Miller (2016) *The CIA and the Congress for Cultural Freedom in the Early Cold War*, Abingdon, Oxon: Routledge

Jakarta Globe (2012) Singapore building camera network despite 'Big Brother' society worries, 20 April. Available online at http://jakartaglobe.id/archive/singapore-building-camera-network-despite-big-brother-society-worries/, accessed on 25 April 2012

Kahn, Gabe (2012) Google set to replace government as Big Brother, *Arutz Sheva*, 25 January. Available online at http://www.israelnationalnews.com/News/News.aspx/152100, accessed on 27 February 2012

Li, Jia-tung (2005) *Uncle Li's Favorite Forty Books*, Taipei: Yuan Shen Publishing

Miller, Claire Cain and Bosman, Julie (2011) E-books outsell print books at Amazon, *New York Times*, 16 May. Available online at http://www.nytimes.com/2011/05/20/technology/20amazon.html, accessed on 20 May 2011

Mirzoeff, Nicolas (1999) *An Introduction to Visual Culture*, London: Routledge

Orwell, George (1986 [1939]) *Coming Up for Air*, Davison, Peter (ed.) *The Complete Works*, London: Secker and Warburg

Orwell, George (1987 [1949]) *Nineteen Eighty-Four*, Davison, Peter (ed.) *The Complete Works*, London: Secker and Warburg

Orwell, George (1950) *Coming Up for Air*, New York: Avon Books

Orwell George (1950) *1984*, New York: Signet Books

Orwell George (1952) *Burmese Days*, New York: Popular Library

Rodden, John (1989) *The Politics of Literary Reputation: The Making and Claiming of 'Saint George Orwell'*, Oxford: Oxford University Press

Rodden, John (2003) *Scenes from an Afterlife: The Legacy of George Orwell*, Wilmington, Delaware: ISI Books

Stone, Brad (2009) Amazon erases Orwell books from Kindle, *New York Times*, 17 July. Available online at http://www.nytimes.com/2009/07/18/technology/companies/18amazon.html, accessed on 1 December 2010

NOTE ON THE CONTRIBUTOR

Henk Vynckier is Associate Professor in the Department of Foreign Languages and Literatures at Tunghai University in Taichung, Taiwan. He co-edited, with John Rodden, 'Orienting Orwell: Asian and Global Perspectives on George Orwell' (special issue of *Concentric: Literary and Cultural Studies*, March 2014) and his articles and essays have appeared in *History of European Ideas*, *CLC Web: Comparative Literature and Culture*, *Biography: An Interdisciplinary Quarterly*, and *The Wenshan Review of Literature and Culture*, as well as edited collections, including *Sinographies: Writing China* (2008) and *George Orwell Now!* (2015).

PAPER

Orwell the Teacher: Such, Such Were the Joys

TIM CROOK

Orwell's essay 'Such, Such Were the Joys' amounts to an excoriating condemnation of the preparatory school system. The young Eric Arthur Blair graduated from his prep school by scholarship to Eton – regarded as the preeminent elitist institution in British private education. Orwell further denounced many aspects of the private education system of the 1920s and 1930s in his novel A Clergyman's Daughter. *He also took up teaching and private tutoring during the early 1930s. Biographers and writers have reported on what it was like to be taught by him. This paper investigates the significance of Orwell's adventures in education. How credible were his views on teaching and the nature of the education that he received? How good a teacher was he in the context of the professionalisation of teaching at the training colleges of the time? To what extent was his writing on education tantamount to another development of his self-fashioning and transformation from Eric Arthur Blair, child of imperialism, to the democratic socialist writer, George Orwell?*

Keywords: education, Eton, private schools, Thomas Raymont, St Cyprian's, teaching

INTRODUCTION

Orwell made education a key issue in his fictional and essay writing. It was a pervasive issue whenever he challenged the perniciousness of the English class system and criticised the gross inequalities of social injustice he observed in Britain during his lifetime. Orwell declared in his 1936 novel *Keep the Aspidistra Flying*: 'Probably the greatest cruelty one can inflict on a child is to send it to school among children richer than itself' (Orwell 1962 [1936]: 46). This paper will seek to investigate Orwell's experiences of education as a child, adolescent and young man in the private preparatory and British public school system of the early part of the 20th century. These have been a focus of great interest by all his biographers.

The exploration of Orwell and education will extend to the impact, significance and representation of his time at Eton – regarded as the preeminent school for the elite during the period he was there and which retains this status one hundred years later. Orwell's account of his privileged time at Eton is ambiguous. He could tell a woman friend: 'If only I'd been sent to another school, a freer co-educational school, I should have been much happier than at Eton' (Meyers 2001: 45). At the same time, he could also agree with a woman he had known in Burma that his ability to show minute care and fairness in dealing with legal disputes and his passion for justice was 'the most important part of the education' he had received at Eton along with 'the capacity to think for myself' (ibid: 46).

Then there is the significance of Orwell as a teacher in private tutoring and classroom instruction at private schools he worked at during the early 1930s in West London. His mischief in teaching his students how to make and detonate bombs (Shelden 1992: 156) and popularity with pupils when working as a schoolmaster at a small private school in Hayes was tempered by the fact that he would exercise an authoritarian streak and beat those who misbehaved severely – leaving at least one boy with 'really bad bruises' and unable to sit down comfortably for a week (Wadhams 1984: 53-54). But Orwell's use of corporal punishment as a teacher was very much out of step with the prevailing culture at the country's leading teacher training college. Leading educationalists at Goldsmiths College, University of London, had been practising a much more progressive pedagogical professionalism from 1905. This exposes Orwell as the product and practitioner of anachronistic methods.

In the wider context, Orwell as the social democratic writer could be reflective about the inadequacies and shortcomings of his educational experiences as Eric Arthur Blair. But he was by no means an original or pioneer thinker in this area. Individuals at Goldsmiths with genuine working class backgrounds, who had won a much more challenging struggle in educational attainment and expertise, put their theory into action many decades before he would write his essay 'Such, Such Were the Joys'. They included, Thomas Raymont, the second Warden (head) of Goldsmiths who was one of thirteen children born to a Devonshire farrier and blacksmith in the Victorian age, and started his educational career as a boy teacher at the age of 13 (Raymont and Scupham 2012: 45-65). By the time he joined the new teacher training department of Goldsmiths in 1905 at the age of 41, he had gained Bachelor's and Master's degrees from the University of London and a Professorship in Education from University College, Cardiff, following the publication of his influential book, *The Principles of Education* in 1904 (ibid).

Raymont's later book *Modern Education: Its Aims and Method* (1931) and publication by his Goldsmiths colleague Nancy Catty of *A First Book On Teaching* (1929), and her edited volume *Modern*

Education of Young Children (1933), demonstrate that Orwell expressed no clear conception and understanding of the developing professional standards of modern education being advanced in the wider public and private sectors of education during his time as a pupil and teacher. It was a Goldsmiths lecturer, J. H. Wimms, who wrote and published the standard textbook, *An Introduction to Psychology For the Use of Teachers*, in 1908 some three years before the eight-year-old Eric Arthur Blair entered St. Cyprian's in Eastbourne.

Orwell's references were from an elitist, male dominated world. Women educationalists such as Alice Woods were charting a wider transformation of progress in teaching. She was able to declare with some optimism in her 1920 book *Educational Experiments in England* that 'Freedom is likely to be brought about in the teaching profession itself. Some form of autonomy will probably take the place of perpetual government direction. The head masters and head mistresses will be free to carry out plans of development for their schools' (Woods 1920: 244).

ST. CYPRIAN'S – 'SUCH, SUCH WERE THE JOYS'

It was his fellow St. Cyprian's and Eton compatriot Cyril Connolly who probably inspired Orwell to write the *J'accuse* of all bitter recollections of prep school days. D. J. Taylor dubbed the Orwellian diatribe as 'one of the most damning indictments of an educational system ever committed to paper' (Taylor 2003: 29). Connolly had sent him a copy of his volume *Enemies of Promise* (1988 [1938]) which, in chapter 19 'White Samite', profiled the pseudonymous St Wulfric's as a school 'well run and vigorous example which did me a world of good' (ibid: 174). Connolly had a broader view of what he had gained and lost in going to a school 'typical of England before the last war; it was worldly and worshipped success, political and social; though Spartan, the death rate was low, for it was well run and based on that stoicism which characterized the English governing class and which has since been under-estimated' (ibid: 175).

But Connolly's account was by no means eulogistic to the bountiful gifts of enlightenment bestowed upon him by the proprietors Leslie and Cecily Wilkes whom, like Orwell, he had characterised in his account by their nicknames of Sambo and Flip. He recalled Flip's propensity when angry 'to slap our faces in front of the school or pull the hair behind our ears, till we cried. She would make satirical remarks at meals that pierced like a rapier' (ibid: 177). Connolly described the humiliating manipulation of her boys by 'spinning them' in and out of favour as if in an 'Elizabeth and Essex relationship' and she was 'hotting them up like little Alfa-Romeos for the Brooklands of life' (ibid).

With writing of that quality, it was not at all surprising that George Orwell was inspired to write an essay based on his traumatic memory of his time at St. Cyprian's. In a letter to Connolly in 1938, he said: 'I wonder how you can write about St. Cyprian's. It's all like an awful nightmare to me, & sometimes I think I can still taste the porridge (out of those pewter bowls do you remember?)' (Davison 1998a: 175). Later that year, Orwell, in another letter to Connolly, described Mrs Wilkes as 'that filthy old sow' and gave notice that 'I'm always meaning one of those days to write a book about St Cyprian's' (ibid: 254).

What he did write about his time there between 1911 and 1916 was a complex and disturbing expression of hatred for the couple who ran a school that prepared him successfully for scholarships to two of the world's most famous private schools: Wellington and Eton. They are confusingly called 'public' schools in British culture because of their origin, many centuries before they achieved their elite status, as charitable foundations set up to educate the able children of the poor. Mr and Mrs Wilkes admitted him for half fees. She was an excellent French teacher and has been credited with guiding the young Eric Blair in the 'crystal pane style' of clear and lucid English that became the hallmark of his writing (Bowker 2003: 34). Bowker said rather pointedly in his biography: 'Her more admiring pupils recalled her great insistence on simplicity and clarity in prose, the very qualities George Orwell later sought to emulate, and he had to admit in certain ways she encouraged him' (ibid).

But overall Orwell was damning, writing: 'I hated Sambo and Flip, with a sort of shamefaced, remorseful hatred' (Davison 1998b: 366). The main source of his bitterness was his belief that they discriminated against him because of his scholarship status and their imposition of a regime of humiliation that included rationing his pocket money, denying him the privilege of ever having a birthday cake, and not even passing on ten shillings his parents had sent for him to buy a cricket bat – something he so desperately wanted. All the while he observed how the rich boys were spared the ghastly floggings and enjoyed special privileges including mid-morning milk and biscuits. He resented being 'crammed with learning as cynically as a goose is crammed for Christmas' (ibid: 360-361). In addition to the physical abuse, Orwell lamented most intensely the psychological torture of never feeling that it was ever possible to be good. He recalled Flip's ability to search the inner core of his conscience 'with her baleful eyes' and her 'peculiar, wheedling, bullying style' (ibid: 364).

Orwell could recall word-for-word thirty years later how he would be assailed with verbal putdowns such as 'He wants to be a little office boy at forty pounds a year', 'I don't think it's very straight, the way you are behaving' and 'You are living on my bounty'. He accused the school of squalor and neglect, of forcing him to exert himself physically when he was afflicted with bronchial illness, of imposing an almost punitive environment of hard beds, and a Spartan diet so limited the children plundered scraps left over from masters' dinners.

He was all too aware that this essay was, in 1948, 'really too libellous to print' (ibid: 356). The first version was published in the US *Partisan Review* in 1952 and it could not be read in British publication until after the death of Mrs Wilkes in 1967. It is hardly surprising when he conjured a world of sour porridge, slimy water, damp towels with cheesy smells, a human turd floating during a swimming lesson, dilapidated and banging lavatory doors without fastenings, and forks with old food between the prongs. Orwell described St. Cyprian's as an evil-smelling compound where periodically boys would hear the 'long, desolate wails' and howling of other boys ringing through the house while being flogged for group masturbation, or other beastly sins that had corrupted the temple of their bodies.

Orwell's biographers have subjected 'Such, Such Were the Joys' to detailed investigation. Bernard Crick referred to a contemporary St. Cyprianite who claimed that the bed-wetter publicly beaten was another boy who went on to become a colonel in the British army and Victoria Cross holder (Crick 1982:69). Crick quoted extensively from the Blair family portfolio of happy letters that Eric sent home during his boarding days in Eastbourne, and concluded: '… if he intended it to be literally truthful, then memory played him some curious tricks, but none the less it was a brilliant polemic – not entirely about the past' (ibid: 80). Other biographers (such as Bowker 2003, Colls 2013, Meyers 2001, Shelden 1992) found as many St. Cyprian's old boys who thought the essay had inflicted a cruel injustice on Mr and Mrs Wilkes as those who corroborated and backed up Orwell's vicious denunciation.

Cyril Connolly regretted blithely mocking the Wilkes when he later discovered family papers showing how much they had genuinely helped him get his scholarship to Eton and surmised Mrs Wilkes 'was warm-hearted and an inspired teacher. The worldliness and snobbery of the Wilkes which Orwell so much condemns was characteristic of the competitive middle class of the period, not a singular aberration' (ibid 98).

Michael Shelden located a memoir by an old boy, Walter Christie, who was also on half fees, and strongly challenged Orwell's characterisation: 'It reminded me of a cobra discharging its self-generated venom by spitting at a harmless tree whose roots had sheltered it' (Shelden 1992: 31). Shelden argues that the true significance of Orwell's essay is that he strove to articulate the impressions and feelings of his boyhood, a 'time when he lacked the articulate voice to speak up for himself' (ibid: 35). But this creative recollection of the past would be intensively controversial and hurtful to the targets of his vituperation. Mr and Mrs Wilkes's eldest son, John, was a contemporary of Orwell at St. Cyprian's during the First World War and later Eton. He dismissed the Orwell diatribe as nonsense and explained the charge of boys being hungry as a situation where 'dash it all, so was everybody, whether they were at school or anywhere else. Everything was rationed' (Wadhams 1984: 11). All photographs of the boys at the time present well-nourished, healthy and happy looking faces. Orwell had no experience of the real poverty, malnutrition, and stunted development of pupil teachers entering Goldsmiths College before the First World War. The college's archives for 1907-1908 reveal a crisis in the state of health of a significant proportion of new 18-year-old trainee teachers: 'As in previous years, a considerable number of otherwise acceptable candidates showed defects of eyesight which were either not corrected, or not adequately corrected, by spectacles; and a still larger number had defective and neglected teeth' (Goldsmiths Archive 1907). It was not unknown for student teachers as late as the 1930s to do their training in local schools in Deptford, south east London, where children were without shoes.

ETON

Jeffrey Meyers observed that Eton gave Orwell what prep school had 'notably failed to provide: freedom, leisure, stimulating classmates, lively teachers, a civilized environment and a cubicle of his own' (Meyers 2001: 27). It was a time to be relaxed and self-possessed. Again, there would be a clear contradiction between the construction of being poor and disadvantaged and the evidence of his friends and contemporaries; one of whom, Sir Steven Runciman said: 'No, he wasn't this embittered boy at school where he was the poorest of all the pupils, longing to get away and too poor to go up to university. I think that's all fictitious' (Wadhams 1984: 20). Meyers depicts a time of intellectual swagger, when he could develop a character described by Runciman as 'a rather sardonically cheerful sort of boy – I mean loving the irony, loving to have a slight grievance against masters and older boys, but enjoying it' (ibid). Meyers reports: 'The indolent, cocky and rather bolshy Eric inevitably clashed with the more overbearing and uncongenial masters' (Meyers 2001: 41).

John Newsinger has a clear view on Eric Arthur Blair's educational trajectory via Eton as 'the product of the Imperial administrative middle class, brought up, educated and indoctrinated to take his place in its ranks' (Newsinger 1999: 1). For Newsinger, St. Cyprian's was 'one of many "cradle and crèche" of Empire schools' (ibid). And the young Eric Blair's sojourn of cynical awkward squad character development at Eton did not divert him from that path.

TIM CROOK

Newsinger observes that his decision to become an officer of the Indian Imperial Police, adhering loyally to the family tradition, was 'hardly the action of a member of the awkward squad' (ibid 2).

That was the purpose of the Etonian elitist process then. It is argued that Eton's dominance in the educational sphere prevails today. It continues to be referred to by alumni as 'School' with an arrogant presumption that the concept of 'school' does not have any equivalent validity anywhere else. According to old boy Will Buckley, Eton endures as a con trick that will run and run. He defines the successful inculcation of inner confidence: 'If you are told regularly enough that you are at a school for excellence then you are likely to leave believing you can achieve anything' (Buckley 2016).

George Woodcock decided Orwell had a double-standard in his attitude to education (Woodcock 1970: 216). Orwell wrote in the *Observer* in 1948 that Eton's great virtue was 'a tolerant and civilized atmosphere which gives each boy a fair chance of developing his individuality' (ibid 216-217). But Woodcock criticised him for 'an extraordinary passage of rabid anti-scholasticism' in which he praises the workers because 'where "education" touches their own lives they see through it and reject it by a healthy instinct' (ibid). Woodcock offers a further insight into Orwell's educational ambivalence in the revelation of a private discussion he had with him about the future education of his adopted son Richard:

> He did not want to send Richard to a boarding school when he was very young, as had happened to him. On the other hand, in spite of his socialism, he was not impressed with the results of state education, and felt that while the present system lasted, there might be worse places to which a boy could be sent, when he was old enough, than a good public school (ibid 159).

Stansky and Abrahams argue that when Eric Blair left Eton in December 1921 'Eton, it might be said, did not leave him – its mark was upon him, in a certain authority and assurance of manner, as later in the authority and assurance of his prose' (Stansky and Abrahams 1979: 135). Meyers assembled the biographical evidence proving that the young George Orwell could have gone to Oxford or Cambridge University with or without a grant. He emphasises that Blair probably 'rebelled at the thought of university' (Meyers 2001: 44). And Stansky and Abrahams are confident that, had he gone, 'it is permissible to suggest that then there would not have been George Orwell. Not going to university was a decisive part in the making of the writer' (Stanksy and Abrahams 1979: 135).

Running throughout any analysis of George Orwell's attitudes to education must be the questions of precisely who was George

Orwell, how did he think and what did he believe in? Robert Colls tackles these issues head on in *George Orwell: English Rebel*, arguing that what makes Orwell such a difficult subject is that in 'his old school slang, he was a "scrub": someone who liked to do what is not done' (Colls 2013: 2). Consequently, George Orwell would be preoccupied with depicting his educational heritage as the victim of a totalitarian culture that had lied to him and bullied him as a snotty, smelly and unloved inferiority. Yet St. Cyprian's educated Eric Arthur Blair to win a scholarship at arguably the most prestigious school in the world. Blair was there because he was clever and Colls poignantly suggests: 'Whatever else we learn of Eric Arthur Blair, we should remember his natural gifts' (ibid 13). While at Eton he earned the right to wear flannels and it 'afforded him some measure of independence which over the years grew into a mild delinquency' (ibid: 14).

Colls concludes that it is never clear that Orwell and Blair are the same man. He decides George Orwell 'is the decent Englishman who goes into corners, puts himself to the test, and can be relied upon to speak the truth, or try to' (ibid: 41). He defines Blair as 'more like the writer Orwell left behind … [who] knows what he wants before he finds it' (ibid). He accepts that over time Blair and Orwell grew inwards together, but it was also possible 'that he never did rid himself of the basic split in who he was and who he wanted to be and, indeed, drew on it for insight and empathy' (ibid 42).

PRIVATE TUTORING AND TEACHING IN WEST LONDON

Bernard Crick quoted at great length the affectionate remembrance of Professor Richard Peters having Eric Arthur Blair as a private tutor when a schoolboy in Southwold in 1930: 'He was a mine of information on birds, animals, and the heroes of boys' magazines. … But of all the activities which we indulged in with him, the one that stands out in my memory most is the making of bombs' (Crick 1982: 209-210). Blair spent so much time blowing up various parts of his tutee's garden that they coined a kind of war cry 'Blarry Boy for Bolshie Bombs', 'Blarry Boy' having become Mr Blair's somewhat irreverent nickname. In 1932, after several years of dossing and writing, the emergent George Orwell taught in two private schools in West London. He had neither a degree nor teaching qualification though they still employed him because of the prestige of his famous former school and posh accent. Colls says: 'They were just about the worst places on earth Orwell could have chosen to work in' (Colls 2013: 35). The exhaustion of doing his best for his students and striving to write his next novel probably contributed to pneumonia and the end of his teaching career. What Orwell saw as high profit racketeering in private middle-class schooling would inform his rather Dickensian depiction of Mrs Creevy's Ringwood House in his novel *A Clergyman's Daughter*, where the medium paying parents would have children whose ears were twisted because they left no marks. Mrs Creevy's advice to her new teacher Dorothy on how to punish the children of bad payers was: 'I don't care what you do to that lot – well, short of a police-court case, naturally' (Orwell 1964 [1936]: 181-182).

One of his former pupils, Geoffrey Stevens, said of Orwell: 'Without a shadow of doubt he was the best teacher I remember at the school. … Whether it was handwork or natural history, he would wholeheartedly support a boy and try to teach him' (Wadhams 1984: 51-52). In this account, Orwell was clearly a popular and enthusiastic teacher of natural history, animals, insects, plants, painting, with French lessons only in French, and who took the trouble to lead children on long, educational country walks. This sounds like a progressive ethos set against the contemporary writing of Thomas Raymont who, in *Modern Education: Its Aims and Methods*, was arguing: 'The fundamental change that has taken place is that the new freedom has made possible the exorcism of the spirit of slavery and the substitution of the spirit of comradeship and discipleship. Plays, concerts magazines, camps and all that makes school a great piece of team work' (Raymont 1931: 270).

But Stevens also reported that Orwell 'was pretty strict and rather harsh … he kept a rule on his desk … he would prod us in the stomach … we had six of the best. I remember I couldn't sit down on it for at least a week. They were really bad bruises. I had a job to sit in the bath, I remember … pretty unjust for such a trivial complaint' (Wadhams 1984: 53-54). Such brutality in the classroom was fast becoming 'a thing of the past' (Raymont 1931: 271). It was the kind of regular punishment and chastisement expected in the Royal Naval School in New Cross that Goldsmiths College had occupied during the 19th century. The college's first woman Vice-President, Caroline Graveson, recalled how, in her first year in 1905, she had been horrified when a former Royal Naval School pupil entered her office to describe how he had been flogged there. She said: 'I wanted to disinfect the room!' after he left (Dymond 1955: 94). In a speech to an educational conference in 1938, Graveson's colleague, Nancy Catty, said: 'Rewards were, indeed, undoubtedly of more use than punishments, as they did achieve something. To punish a child only left him tired or inclined to be resentful. Nobody ever realised after being punished that they deserved their punishment' (*Sevenoaks Chronicle* 1938).

EDUCATION, THE MEDIA, SOCIETY AND THE WIDER CONTEXT

At around the same time it is estimated that Orwell was grinding his antipathy towards St. Cyprian's, he was also writing his cultural assessment of *The English People* for the 'British People in Pictures

Series'. On the penultimate page, bearing an illustration of the modernist 1944 sculpture 'The Family' by Henry Moore, Orwell wrote: '…there is still need for a conscious effort at national re-education. The first step towards this is an improvement in elementary education, which involves not only raising the school-leaving age but spending enough money to ensure that elementary schools are adequately staffed and equipped' (Orwell 1947: 47). His pretence at expertise on matters of educational policy was not based on one day of professional training, or experience in the state education system. There is no evidence that he would have been aware that in 1933 Nancy Catty's edited volume on *Modern Education of Young Children* was advancing analysis of the transition from formal teaching to project work and methods by which children, free to play singly or in groups, were gaining general education and rapidly acquiring skill in the three Rs. Mrs Catty and her colleagues were putting into practice the theory of the free child in the child-centred school: 'There are many attempts made to counteract the evils of the formal work that often follows in the wake of the time-table, the fixed syllabus, the rule of the specialist and the tyranny of the examination' (Catty 1933: ix).

To be fair to Orwell, there were concessions of grudging balance in 'Such, Such Were the Joys'. He accepted: 'Whoever writes about his childhood must beware of exaggeration and self-pity. I do not want to claim that I was a martyr or that St. Cyprian's was a sort of Dotheboys Hall' (Davison 1998b: 396). His essay was recollecting and polemicising education 'thirty years ago and more' and he was seeking to ask the question: 'Does a child at school go through the same kind of experiences nowadays?' (ibid: 382). Orwell accepted that there was a prevailing attitude towards education that was 'enormously more humane and sensible than that of the past' (ibid: 383). He somewhat patronisingly observed 'a general growth of "enlightenment" even among ordinary, unthinking middle-class people' (ibid). He hoped that the domination of religious belief had vanished, beating had been discredited and largely abandoned from many schools and 'I imagine that very few people nowadays would tell a child that if it masturbates it will end up in the lunatic asylum' (ibid).

Orwell's thinking also turned to the educational significance of the media when he talked of 'immense educational possibilities in the radio, the film, and – if it could be freed once and for all from commercial interests – the press' (Orwell 1947: 47). Sarah Lonsdale situates this view in the atmosphere of intense criticism of press ethics and plurality that was accompanied and followed by the Royal Commission into the Press in 1948. She says this most likely contributed to the dystopian depiction of fabricated news production in *Nineteen Eighty-Four*:

TIM CROOK

Some of the most resounding criticisms of the British press submitted to the inquiry focused on its failure to fulfil its most fundamental duty in a liberal democracy: to help produce, through articulating divergent views of public opinion, an enlightened public which could conduct its civic duty in full knowledge of events (Lonsdale 2016: 162).

Yet profound understanding of the impact on education that a competitive and superficial media had on the minds of schoolchildren had been publicly ventilated more than twenty years before by Goldsmiths College Warden Thomas Raymont. The *Dover Express* reported his sophisticated understanding of media effects when he said the press, as an educational medium, had to be reckoned with by teachers. Raymont warned against 'the new journalism' with its emphasis on the 'daily triviality and its avoidance of all that related to permanent principles in ethics, economics, and politics' (*Dover Express* 1925: 5). Raymont appreciated the more sophisticated involvement of teachers utilising 'improvements in the education of boys and girls over 12 years of age as would make it possible for them to read with greater discrimination as they grew up. Then, and not till then, would the newspapers improve' (ibid).

CONCLUSION

George Orwell was both a very good and very bad teacher who never had any ambition to commit his life to education. His mission in life after returning from imperial service as a policeman in Burma was to become a writer. Periods of private tutoring and jobs in private schools in West London played important parts in the making of Orwell the writer. For in the process, he collected intense and poignant experience to inform some of his novels of the 1930s such as *A Clergyman's Daughter*.

He was a good teacher, inspiring the imagination and curiosity of his pupils with the wonders of nature, though the instruction he offered in showing young people how to cause explosions would be regarded as somewhat irresponsible today. There is no doubt he was committed to his students. The exhaustive work in devising and producing drama productions made him aware that extra-curricular commitments diverted him from the necessary energy and focus needed to succeed as a writer. He had clearly been conditioned by the brutal punishment techniques at St. Cyprian's and Eton to beat and physically intimidate children under his care. Though this widespread abuse may have been standard in the private schools of the 1930s, it was regarded as anachronistic and unprofessional in the leading training colleges for teachers going into state schools.

Orwell had no clear insight or appreciation of the many gifts and advantages that the hated teachers at St. Cyprian's had given him. Equally, he was rather off-hand about how the privileges and opportunities of Eton had propelled and advanced him in the elite milieu. Skills, knowledge, confidence, contacts, tenacity, cunning and even a powerfully inculcated perspicacity of writing style had been invested in a young man who would go on to be one of the most influential novelists and political writers of his century. Eton essentially gave him the space to develop as an individual thinker.

Although Orwell was disconnected and not fully grounded in the progressive developments taking place in professional education, he must be credited with having a fundamental emotional understanding of how children feel and experience education that is not working for them. 'Such, Such Were the Joys' has passages of insight that have been often overlooked by his biographers so engaged with the mythology of the young Orwell as Oliver Twist, Tom Brown, or Dotheboys Hall victim. In the concluding pages of the essay, he questioned 'whether it is still normal for a schoolchild to live for years amid irrational terrors and lunatic misunderstandings' (Davison 1998b: 383). He acknowledged the difficulty for adults to know what a child actually thinks and feels. There is great sensitivity and sympathy expressed in the observation: 'A child which appears reasonably happy may actually be suffering horrors which it cannot or will not reveal. It lives in a sort of alien under-water world which we can only penetrate by memory or derivation' (ibid). Mrs Cecily Wilkes was utterly perplexed by Orwell's denunciation. Her son John recalled that 'she had a great respect for him and was very much hurt when he said the things about the school he did' (Wadhams 1984: 10). Biographer D. J. Taylor argues that the dark depiction of St. Cyprian's as a miserable penal colony may have had something to do with the fact that the essay was written during the conception and development of *Nineteen Eighty-Four*: 'The idea of the school as a police state, Mrs Wilkes with her arbitrary favouritism – all this, it could be said, is the mental baggage of *Nineteen Eighty-Four* shifted back in time' (Taylor 2003: 35). Certainly, Orwell's first biographer Bernard Crick considered if he was 'transfiguring imaginatively aspects of his early experiences into what was soon to become the helplessness of Winston Smith' (Crick 1982: 71).

A critical view of Orwell would suggest that he was clever at exploiting all the advantages of his elitist and imperialist privileges to enter (and, in some respects, ultimately dominate) the world of writers. Was he too selfish to be a good teacher? Great writers often are. It is easy to be a tramp and live for a while with the poor when you have comfortable bourgeois friends and family who can lend a bath, bed and refuge.

Eric Arthur Blair's success as the author 'George Orwell' depended on rebelling against the authoritative and effective education given to him. At St. Cyprian's he had an education in animosity, grievance, unfairness and bullying. At Eton, he gained a diploma in

PAPER

cynicism. When he worked as a teacher, he could equivocate with orthodox and unorthodox methods. When he was fully developed as a writer, his remarkable prose and essays achieved precisely what he wanted – making political writing a unique art form.

REFERENCES

Bowker, Gordon (2003) *George Orwell*, London: Little Brown

Buckley, Will (2016) The big Eton con trick will run and run – don't let it fool you, *Guardian*, 5 September. Available online at https://www.theguardian.com/commentisfree/2016/sep/05/eton-con-trick-eu-vote-etonian-prime-ministers-school, accessed on 1 September 2017

Catty, Nancy, Roe, Frances and Boyce, E. R. (1933) *Modern Education of Young Children*, London: Methuen & Co. Ltd

Catty, Nancy (1950) *A First Book on Teaching*, London: Methuen & Co. Ltd, fifth edition

Colls, Robert (2013) *George Orwell: The English Rebel*, Oxford: Oxford University Press

Crick, Bernard (1982) *George Orwell: A Life*, Harmondsworth: Penguin Books, second edition

Connolly, Cyril (1988 [1938]) *Enemies of Promise*, London: Andre Deutsch

Davison, Peter (ed.) (1998a) *The Complete Works of George Orwell, Volume 11: Facing Unpleasant Facts 1937-1939*, London: Secker & Warburg

Davison, Peter (ed.) (1998b) *The Complete Works of George Orwell, Volume 19: It is What I Think 1947-1948*, London: Secker & Warburg

Dover Express (1925) Naming of Teachers, 14 August p. 5

Dymond, Dorothy (ed.) (1954) *The Forge: The History of Goldsmiths' College*, London: Methuen & Co. Ltd

Goldsmiths, University of London, Special Collections and Archives, Annual Report of Delegacy 1907-1908

Lonsdale, Sarah (2016) *The Journalist in British Fiction & Film: Guarding the Guardians from 1900 to the Present*, London: Bloomsbury Academic

Meyers, Jeffrey (2001) *Orwell: Wintry Conscience of a Generation*, London: W.W. Norton & Company

Newsinger, John (1999) *Orwell's Politics*, Basingstoke: Palgrave

Orwell, George (1947) *The English People*, London: Collins

Orwell, George (1962 [1936]) *Keep the Aspidistra Flying*, Harmondsworth: Penguin Books

Orwell, George (1964 [1936]) *A Clergyman's Daughter*, Harmondsworth: Penguin Books

Raymont, Thomas (1913) *The Principles of Education*, London: Longmans, Green and Co., third edition

Raymont, Thomas (1935) *Modern Education: Its Aims And Methods*, London: Longmans, Green and Co.

Raymont, Thomas and Scupham, Carola (2012) *From Blacksmith to Goldsmiths*, Hitchin: Olive Press

Sevenoaks Chronicle and Kentish Advertiser (1938) Rewards and punishments, Educational Limpsfield, 10 June p. 5

Shelden, Michael (1992) *Orwell: The Authorised Biography*, London: Minerva

Stansky, Peter and Abrahams, William (1974) *The Unknown Orwell*, London: Paladin Grafton Books

Stansky, Peter and Abrahams, William (1979) *Orwell: The Transformation*, London: Constable

Taylor, D. J. (2003) *Orwell: The Life*, London: Chatto & Windus

Wadhams, Stephen (1984) *Remembering Orwell*, Harmondsworth: Penguin Books

Wimms, J. H. (1913) *An Introduction to Psychology: For the Use of Teachers*, London: Charles and Son, third edition

Woodcock, George (1970) *The Crystal Spirit: A Study of George Orwell*, Harmondswoth: Penguin Books

Woods, Alice (1920) *Educational Experiments in England*, London: Methuen & Co.

NOTE ON THE CONTRIBUTOR

Tim Crook is Professor in the Department of Media and Communications at Goldsmiths, Visiting Professor in Broadcast Journalism at Birmingham City University, chair of the Professional Practices Board of the Chartered Institute of Journalists and a longstanding author, playwright and academic. He has written a number of academic articles and chapters on George Orwell's literature and cultural significance and is completing a monograph on *Orwell on the Radio* for Ashgate.

PAPER

ARTICLE

Orwell's Children: Fighting for Voice

JON PRESTON

Jon Preston draws on his experience of teaching to show how studying Animal Farm *can help students discover their authentic voices.*

In an era of homogenised culture and digitised knowledge, it can be difficult to access authentic examples of voice. Young people often seem glued to mobile phones, their portable social and cultural nerve-centres. Increasingly their parents do too. Indeed, at a time of Snapchat and Instagram, what chance is there for the well-crafted word or the considered thought? Are we not facing a crisis in voice?

And Orwell's warning in *Nineteen Eighty-Four* (1949) reverberates: 'Who controls the past controls the future: who controls the present controls the past.'

However, there are some tales of encouragement to be found. One such beacon resides in the form of the BRIT School for the Performing Arts and Technology, a state-funded arts school in south London – 100 yards east of the Selhurst railway depot and 100 yards south of the Crystal Palace football stadium. I have been working at 'the BRIT' for twenty years. This article presents an account of some of that work – and, hopefully, offers some hope.

In the broadest sense, I consider myself and my generation to be 'children of Orwell'. His writing has been an integral part of our growth. Discovering *Nineteen Eighty-Four* as a teenager gave voice to the world into which I was growing, in my case south London of the 1970s and 1980s. That feeling of unease I felt when confronted by riots in Brixton or various policing scandals, for example during the miners' strike of 1984-1985 or later, in the Stephen Lawrence case.

As my political sense developed, I became more aware of the disconnection between the powerful media version of events and the voices one could seek out through alternative sources. Thus Orwell's laying-bare the ways in which an oppressive state or an oppressive hierarchy could monitor, control and finally snuff out dissident or independent thought struck a chord with me. That book, now almost 70 years old, is still a litmus paper against which to measure our individual freedoms or lack thereof. As a teenager, Orwell empowered me with a vocabulary that helped me to name what I was observing. As a grown-up, it still serves to remind me that we are engaged in an ongoing struggle for the independent voice.

PRESSURES TO CONFORM

It's hard to be independent. There is always pressure to conform. I feel it hugely as a secondary school teacher, with reams of meaningless data and target-chasing taking time away from my teaching, my creativity, but keeping me in a job in this most unsure of economic climates. Managers love the data because they think it provides easy answers to questions they may have, or more likely be asked of them by someone else. And so it goes on. It's hugely time-consuming and offers little in return. I try to shelter my students from it as best I can because I aim to create an environment in which they can develop their own voices, a process that takes time. I also try to encourage their reading. After all, through his writing, I was able access Orwell's ideas, to 'hear his voice', and I want them to be able to do the same. Indeed, I encourage them to seek out a range of voices on the journey to developing their own. Thus, in a modest way, I aim to create and sustain an 'alternative site for voice'. An alternative to 'Snapchats', Instagram and the other channels of communication on offer to our young people; and to the sound-bites of a predominantly conformist, mainstream media diet. In the classroom I aim to offer a place where young people can practise using their voices and then, through the school radio station, I aspire to takes things up a notch.

I have recently completed a practice-based PhD at Goldsmiths, University of London, called 'Voice in Radio' and it's about my radio projects with socially-marginalised groups. The participants make the journey from hearing their own voices back, often for the first time, right through to sharing their stories in radio programmes aired on the school radio station and shared with their families and friends. I should mention that Brit FM offers a platform for many other voices to be heard. Broadcasting for ten days each summer, as many as 100 broadcasters make programmes that are transmitted online live and then replayed in rotation for some months afterwards. Local primary school children, BRIT School students and staff and community groups all get involved. They have control over content and to hear them is a joy. It is unusual to encounter such a range of voices on a radio station, any radio station. It offers an alternative to what's out there.

JON PRESTON

In *Why Voice Matters: Culture and Politics after Neo-Liberalism* (London: Sage, 2010), Nick Couldry identifies what he calls 'a crisis in voice': in other words, 'neo-liberalism' makes mainstream outlets for self-expression and political dissent very limited. Moreover, the notion that such thought is valid, worthwhile, important, even the idea of 'voice' itself is specifically undermined by neo-liberal ideologies (ibid: 82).

My drive, then, in response, is to create and nurture 'alternative sites for voice', whether in the classroom or on the school radio station. It's about developing the independent, original thinkers, writers, artists, scientists, climate change activists, even party politicians of tomorrow. And in my view, current orthodoxies don't do that. Happily, I think there are many of us creating and maintaining alternative sites for voice in our own way. To that end, we are all 'Orwell's children'. I also see and hear plenty of examples of authentic voice coming through the ether, whether it's a fine screenwriter for a TV show or an independent documentary film-maker or a musician who has connected with an audience; or a young person who has simply tired of seeing his friends stabbed to death and chosen to speak out. But none of that is easy. You have to fight for your voice. One way or another, you have to fight to be heard, particularly if you are challenging orthodoxies. And so, as Orwell's children, we fight for Voice.

At this point, I'd like to introduce some new voices. Firstly, through a piece written by a participant from a homeless group I worked with recently. They learned radio production skills and then worked with students at the school to produce radio shows. This group was from a hostel organisation that works with the homeless to give them skills, work-placements and, hopefully, move them on to independent living. As part of the radio work, they produced poems. Here is a young woman called Shelbie:

A POEM WITHOUT A HOME
Without a home, without a hope,
Trying hard to struggle and cope,
Struggling through the cold at night,
Holding on with all your might,
No soap, no gel, no water to bathe,
Feeling as though you belong in a cave.
Remember, homelessness has no criteria,
Never feel the homeless are inferior.
Homelessness does not just affect me
But thousands across London city.

READING ALOUD *ANIMAL FARM*

Let's now go on into a classroom and you can meet some more children of Orwell. Away from the radio I've also taught GCSE English at the BRIT for many years, always with the lowest set which comprises students who struggle with literacy. We study set texts that include *Macbeth* and *Pride and Prejudice*. These are both great works but they are quite a difficult read for some of these students. We also had John Steinbeck's *Of Mice and Men* until a former education secretary, Michael Gove, took it out of the syllabus. That was a book-crime. However, we do still have George Orwell's *Animal Farm*.

One of the issues for these students is reading aloud, so I rearrange the classroom, move the desks and get them all sat round in a circle. I call it, originally enough, 'the reading circle'. Everyone takes a turn to read. No-one laughs or sniggers if someone stumbles over a word and, gradually, these students find their reading voices. I always think that, regardless of their final GCSE grade or their 'target attainment grade', if these students are empowered to read to their own children one day, should they be blessed that way, then I have done my job. The management and the data police might not agree but I know the students get it.

I've seen the reading circle work well. I want you to hear from a boy who really struggled to read aloud for a long time. Let's hear from Connor.

CONNOR

C: Before I started at the BRIT my confidence in reading wasn't... great. At the start in Year 10, I was not confident at all. I would never really want to read out loud...

J: What do you remember about the reading circle that we used to do in the class?

C: Yeah, the reading circle ... that really helped with my reading because ... it was a case of everyone would *have* to read. It wouldn't be like a lot but it would be like a couple of pages and then we'd switch over, but that really helped because within the circle we would hear people's voices and we would see them reading instead of just sitting at table by table, in a classroom looking at the books or heads down on the table listening to someone read.

J: What do you remember about reading *Animal Farm* in the reading circle?

C: It made me understand the story a lot more, reading in the reading circle with *Animal Farm* ... and I was quite drawn into that. Because I would be so stuck into what other people were reading, how they would read it and how they would interpret the book themselves…

J: What can you remember about *Animal Farm* that caught your attention?

C: It was just animals acting like humans … it was such an unusual thing … and within the reading circle again … some people would put on accents, just have a laugh … that's just what drew my attention, because they're animals acting like humans. It was unusual and funny.

J: Do you think he's a good writer and if so, why?

C: Yeah, I think Orwell … he is an amazing writer because he doesn't just write … to get people's attention. He writes … as things *are*.

J: What do you mean by that?

C: Because… I dunno, I just like the way he structures it and … say like in the reading circle when I was reading for instance, I would be able to read what he was saying and be able to understand what he was saying … he wouldn't use big words that people weren't able to understand … it'd be understandable for … older people … and younger people as well … so, yeah, I just think his writing's really easy to understand.

J: Are you reading anything at the moment?

C: Erm…I haven't really been reading anything recently because of all the work within my Theatre Strand … but I've been reading quite a few scripts, like Shakespeare and contemporary scripts as well, so I've done quite a bit of reading this year.

J: Is reading important to you and if so, why?

C: Yes, reading is *very* important to me and I'd say it's important to me because I want to be an actor and to be an actor obviously you need to be good at reading … and I think reading, it's just one of the most important things because if I didn't have the confidence to read and if I still had major troubles reading then it would hold me back from being a great actor…

J: …which is what you're gonna be

C: Which is…yeah, hopefully…
(both laugh)

Connor is an example of a student whose literacy improved significantly through reading aloud in a circle with his classmates. Let me give you the data on that, by the way. It takes about ten minutes to set up and ten minutes to pack down, to get the tables out of the way and the chairs re-arranged. That's twenty minutes out of a two-hour session. In case the data police tell you that's a whole twenty minutes the kids aren't learning, I could respond by saying that the setting-up and packing-down together is an integral part of the process. The students are investing in the reading circle as a group. And you know it's working when they get it down to five minutes each way, which is pretty impressive, because they want to get on and read; they want to find out what happened next in *Animal Farm*.

FINDING ELEMENTS OF EMPOWERMENT IN MOLLIE

So in my last English group, many of my students learned to read aloud in the reading circle through George Orwell's *Animal Farm*. We had some high old times as they realised things were not going well for the animals. There was plenty of debate over Napoleon, Squealer, Snowball and Mollie, Farmer Jones's trap pony with pretty ribbons who struggles with post-revolutionary Animal Farm. Mollie, who jumps ship by going back to work for the human farmers who treat her better than the pigs. Some of the young women in set S4 quite admired Mollie. They certainly thought she had her head screwed on. 'She's not really a sell-out,' they said, 'more that she's using what little she's got to empower herself as best she can in a patriarchal society. She's fighting for her survival.'

As part of a talk on 'Orwell's Women' at the Goldsmiths Orwell Symposium in 2016, Professor Jean Seaton, of Westminster University, had said that 'no sentient woman could recognise Orwell's portrayal of Mollie as any woman they would recognise…' I could agree with Professor Seaton in her criticisms of Orwell's portrayal of Julia in *Nineteen Eighty-Four*. But when she 'slated' Mollie, I felt compelled to represent the voices of the young women in set S4 so I offered their defence of Mollie to the seminar. It turned out that the man who was craning his neck round a few rows in front of me and nodding enthusiastically in agreement was Richard Blair, son of George Orwell.

The next morning in double English, when we had set up the reading circle in five minutes flat, I said: 'A funny thing happened yesterday….' And so I told them about my intervention at the seminar and my punch-line was this: '…And that man nodding vigorously and agreeing with *your* point was George Orwell's son. So you've got a *direct* link to the author of the book we've been reading because not only has his son heard what you think about a character in his dad's book, he's also got a lot of sympathy for your point of view.' For the students in the group that was Big Stuff.

ARTICLE

JON PRESTON

So when Professor Tim Crook asked me back to speak at the 2017 Orwell Seminar, I thought it sensible to take some of those S4 students with me. When it comes to Mollie, they can put it better than me. Gloria Beyi is one of the young women who saw more in Mollie than just the ribbons and the sugar. She performed a spoken-word piece written specifically for the seminar to give voice to that character, Mollie, from George Orwell's *Animal Farm*.

MOLLIE

Life is nothing but ribbons and sugar

When the world drowned in the silly idea of reformation and revolution,

Forget.

You must appreciate what you have in order to remain with the luxuries long-worked for.

Life is nothing but ribbons and sugar

When I, with my silky mare locks engage weak eyes to fall into what some may call a trap

But simply the essence of life

In order for my exploited hoof marks to relieve accusations of galloping and fleeing from labour

Paws with flaws, neighs with a touch of laze, oinks with poise but a closed-eye when it comes to who gets the equal amount of hay.

Life is nothing but a lie

When eyes that once loved you, when sugary cubes once devoured on a daily

Suddenly disappear,

With previous sweats of trying to impress with my extraordinary beauty few notice.

Beauty is a job, you know,

When life is all for getting ribbons and sugar, ignoring bone and soul.

Ask anybody else.

Oh, of course they wouldn't know, because life is nothing but a lie for someone who works on their own.

Limelight is all mine in this forsaken field, credit only I shall claim

As others fool themselves into thinking hard labour concludes into reward.

I'm a profitable prize myself.

Beauty is a job, you know.

Beauty is a job.

It's put me in this business of being an exhibitionist,

With my pretty ribbons and my rewards in sugar.

There were other young women in that set who recognised elements of empowerment in Mollie. They were a group who had shown significant progress after the first year of the course. The data police might have suggested they move up to a higher set. I told those students: 'You're seen as higher-set material now.' They also proved to be children of Orwell. They weren't going to be told. They were going to think for themselves. They all opted to stay put in set S4 and they all did pretty well.

Ashwynna was one of those students, gaining A's in both her English Language and Literature GCSEs. She had been due to speak at the seminar but felt overwhelmed with her post-16 coursework and in the end sent her apologies. Happily I was able to recall two of the points she had made in the preceding week's run-through and offer them to the audience. The first was that, in doing some online research for her talk, she had come across what she described as 'some pretty vitriolic stuff written about George Orwell in relation to his attitudes about women'. Ashwynna had said that, from what she understood of Orwell's views towards humanity, she doubted he could be misogynistic in the way some of these websites had described him. The second was simpler: 'We all know someone like Mollie,' she said.

I'd like to end by bringing Gloria back centre-stage. Here she writes in her own voice:

WO!MAN

What does it mean to be a woman?

To think such question exists.

My femininity runs away from my skeleton to explore

When exactly did disregarding, disrespecting women become so cool?

Being the hot topic of your brethren's mouth due to the uncured diagnosis of pack mentality

Being a woman is when your natural beauty is the front face of your article

Only classified 'literate beings' can only read.

Since being a Wo!man comes with layers of integrity, dignity and possibly pride.

The currency of success and wisdom is experience when it comes to being a woman

With that exact experience comes tears, fears, flaws

and lastly, jaws that engage in speech of discouragement

Woah, Man, tell us,

What have we done that it's not every day sensitive?

That leaves me pensive. What are senses?

JON PRESTON

When I cannot control my intensity of my own *voice*
Since as a woman I live in a world where our voices are mute,
Our patience spread by people who do not love or appreciate us.
This is when I get annoyed, because I understand.
It's not us girls, it's not you boys.
Many think boys do not have feelings,
Not gonna lie, most of those people are boys themselves,
I don't know why you all seem to communicate to each other that you cannot cry,
Cannot feel…anything.
Feeling is man-like.
It's wrong? Feel it like a man.
Touch that pain like a man and also
Indulge and drown in that very same pain
Like a man.
Let us all be a Wo!man.

NOTE ON THE CONTRIBUTOR

Following a decade as a freelance BBC Radio broadcaster and two years on tour with Ska band Bad Manners, Jon Preston recently completed his twentieth year as a teacher at the BRIT School. In his spare time he performs 'outdoor radio' as a festival MC, listens to Ska and Reggae music and plays the trumpet in acoustically pleasing locations. He has recently re-discovered a joy in writing.

ARTICLE

The Rhetoric of Doublethink

PHILIP PALMER

Orwell was a visionary who attacked lies through a 'plain' prose that rang true in every phrase; yet he also used rhetorical strategies with skill and creative guile. He was, in short, a master of his own brand of rhetoric, writes Philip Palmer.

It was a bright cold day in April, and the clocks were striking thirteen. Winston Smith, his chin nuzzled into his breast in an effort to escape the vile wind, slipped quickly through the glass doors of Victory Mansions, though not quickly enough to prevent a swirl of gritty dust from entering along with him (Orwell 1976 [1949]: 743).

The prose is clear, vivid and evocative; the main character is brought to us in all his cowering lack of glory, entering his block of flats. But the word 'thirteen' strikes a dissonant note. It is alienating. It evokes a strange world in which the twenty-four hour clock system is in operation. A future world. A science fictional world.

Nineteen Eighty-Four is a masterpiece of storytelling and world-building, and its vision of a surveillance society in which lies masquerade as truth has never seemed so prescient. At times it is lyrical, even erotic. But more typically, Orwell uses his crisp descriptive style to oppress and to appal. And the appendix on Newspeak is a vital part of the text: for *Nineteen Eighty-Four* is as much a novel about language as it is a story of characters in their world.

There are many forms of language: from abstract poetry that does not have to 'mean' anything except the taste of the word and the tang of the simile, to prose which does a job, and says a thing – prose that makes things happen. One word for such prose is rhetoric and Orwell was a master of it. The purpose of rhetoric is persuasion; it follows, therefore, that all prose which serves the function of rhetoric is a form of propaganda. Orwell embraced this truth proudly. As he asserts, in his essay 'Charles Dickens':

PHILIP PALMER

Every writer, especially every novelist, *has* a 'message', whether he admits it or not, and the minutest details of his work are influenced by it. All art is propaganda. Neither Dickens himself nor the majority of Victorian novelists would have thought of denying this. On the other hand, not all propaganda is art (Orwell 1980 [1940a]: 468, italics in the original).

I would categorise three major types of rhetoric: classical rhetoric, 'banal' rhetoric and Orwellian rhetoric. Classical rhetoric is the rhetoric of Cicero, full of repetition and alliteration and tricks of style. It uses techniques such as *reductio ad absurdum* – mocking an argument by reducing it to its most absurd corollary. Or *argumentum ad hominem* – playing the man, not the ball. The tricks of style associated with this form of rhetoric often have wonderful names, such as *anadiplosis* (repeating the last word of one clause or phrase to begin the next) and *anaphora* (a succession of sentences or clauses beginning with the same word or group of words). This is a classic example of *anaphora* (my emphases):

> **We shall fight** in France, **we shall fight** on the seas and oceans, **we shall fight** with growing confidence and growing strength in the air, we shall defend our island, whatever the cost may be. **We shall fight** on the beaches, **we shall fight** on the landing grounds, **we shall fight** in the fields and in the streets, **we shall fight** in the hills …

This is Prime Minister Winston Churchill's masterly speech (1940) which helped turn the tide of the war by persuading a nation that the monumental defeat at Dunkirk was a kind of victory. It was an act of salesmanship in other words; and every student of language has to admire the art of this old fashioned oratory.

'Banal' rhetoric, however, is the language of the mob, of the rabble rouser. It uses repetition like a fist; it has no elegance; at its crudest, it can be a chant. We have observed a recent example of banal rhetoric in action in Charlottesville, Kentucky, August 2017, in the march upon the statue of Confederate Gen. Robert E. Lee during which a mob chanted 'Blood and soil' and 'Jews will not replace us'. At it worst, banal rhetoric is dishonest, cruel, and ugly; and yet it can be effective.

AYATOLLAH KHOMEINI AND RHETORIC

One of the greatest practitioners of this form of rhetoric – in which language is stripped back to banal, almost childlike levels of vocabulary – was the Iranian scholar and preacher Ayatollah Khomeini. As a young man, Khomeini was known for his complex and profound oratorical style. But in the early 1960s, he became a vocal critic of the Shah of Iran and – according to Ronen Bergman, in his book *The Secret War with Iran* (2008) – he abandoned his previous preaching style and spoke simply, with a vocabulary limited to 2,000 words. As Bergman explains: 'By sheer repetition of certain phrases they took on the nature of magical incantations' (ibid: 9). Furthermore, Khomeini began to portray the world as a clash between good and evil; the evil must be uprooted and destroyed by the good. It was a simple message and therein lay its power.

The Iranian writer Amir Taheri describes an audio-cassette he obtained in the autumn of 1977, ostensibly of a sermon delivered by Khomeini. Taheri thought it was a forgery, created by the Shah's secret police in order to present Khomeini in a ludicrous and grotesque light. It described, in preposterous detail, an imaginary conspiracy between the Shah and the Jews and the Christians with the intent of destroying Islam in Iran.

Taheri was convinced the tape was the work of an actor imitating Khomeini – for how could a man as clever as Khomeini resort to such ludicrous lies? But the recording was authentic. By the end of 1978, more than 600,000 cassettes containing Khomeini's sermons had been distributed in Iran. Each was listened to in groups of at least ten Iranians, so it is estimated that at least six million Iranians out of a population of thirty-six million heard these words. Among the simply worded rants Khomeini uttered in these speeches:

> The despised Shah, that Jewish spy, the American snake, whose head must be crushed with a stone.

> The Shah says that he is giving the people freedom. Listen to me, you puffed up toad! Who are you to grant liberty! It is Allah who grants liberty; it is the law that grants liberty, it is Islam that grants liberty, it is the constitution that grants liberty. What do you mean when you say you have granted us liberty? What gives you the ability to grant anything at all? Who do you think you are? (see Bergman 2008: 11-12).

In 1979, this frail 77-year old returned to Iran from Paris and was received by millions at Tehran's airport. Without a single shot being fired, he defeated the sixth strongest army in the world and became leader of Iran. It was one of the greatest wars in the history of warfare: a war of words. No more than two thousand words, repeated over and over, mixing lies with truth, using repetition like a Gatling gun. Such is the power of banal rhetoric.

ORWELL'S BRAND OF RHETORIC

Thirdly, let us look at Orwell's brand of rhetoric. It is not banal – far from it. Nor is it classical. He scorns overly elaborate prose and erudite diction in favour of a 'plain style'. A journalistic essay-writing style which he exemplifies and which has inspired generations of

PHILIP PALMER authors to write more clearly and, we may hope, more truthfully. Orwell argues, in his essay 'Politics and the English Language', that:

> Most people who bother with the matter at all would admit that the English language is in a bad way, but it is generally assumed that we cannot by conscious action do anything about it. Our civilization is decadent, and our language – so the argument runs – must inevitably share in the general collapse (Orwell 1980 [1946]: 735).

This prose employs a number of rhetorical tricks, not least by stating its thesis, its argument, as an irrefutable conclusion. Most people agree that the English language is in a bad way, Orwell informs us – therefore it is true. Why bother proving it! Later Orwell references an 'argument' he is able to easily dismiss, but does not say who said it. In this way, using snobbish condescension to crush all doubters, Orwell's opinion becomes a truth universally acknowledged. He is not asking for our opinion. He is *compelling* us to adopt *his* views as *our* views. It is a masterly act of rhetorical persuasion.

Orwell then goes on to prove his case, with dazzling skill, by quoting from the works of a number of fairly distinguished writers including Professor Harold Laski. At first glance, these pieces of prose appear to be moderately well written. Orwell, however, humiliates Laski and the others with a series of close analyses, which expose all their terrible style errors:

> Each of these passages has faults of its own but, quite apart from avoidable ugliness, two qualities are common to them all. The first is staleness of imagery: the other is lack of precision. The writer either has a meaning and cannot express it, or he inadvertently says something else, or he is almost indifferent as to whether his words mean anything or not. The mixture of vagueness and sheer incompetence is the most marked characteristic of modern English prose, and especially of any kind of political writing (ibid: 737).

Among the many glaring blunders these lesser writers perpetrate are:

- Dying metaphors. Not fresh and new; but not safely dead either.
- Operators, or verbal false limbs – those words that pad out a sentence but add nothing.
- Pretentious diction.
- The use of meaningless words.

Orwell further proves his case by his spoof paraphrase of a verse from Ecclesiastes. The original reads:

I returned, and saw under the sun, that the race is not to the swift, nor the battle to the strong, neither yet bread to the wise, nor yet riches to men of understanding, nor yet favour to men of skill; but time and chance happeneth to them all.

In the kind of English perpetrated by pompous academics, Orwell suggests, this might read:

Objective consideration of contemporary phenomena compels the conclusion that success or failure in competitive activities exhibits no tendency to be commensurate with innate capacity, but that a considerable element of the unpredictable must invariably be taken into account (ibid: 739).

Thus, through mockery, parody and sheer remorseless attention to detail, Orwell – who never went to university – proves himself to be a better writer than all those distinguished figures he has quoted. And in doing so, he establishes his *authority* over them all. It is this authority, blended with insight and contemptuous rage, that gives his political writings such undeniable power. In the same essay, Orwell points out: 'In our time, it is broadly true that political writing is bad writing' (ibid: 741). The subtext of this (rendered by me in italics) is: all political writing *apart from mine* is bad writing.

Here, Orwell uses a sneer as a warrior uses a sword: to impale or to disembowel. But he does not assert his superiority over other commentators out of mere vanity; he does so in order to vanquish his mortal enemy, that species of monstrous and shameless falsehood which in our age we call 'post-truth':

Political language – and with variations this is true of all political parties, from Conservatives to Anarchists – is designed to make lies sound truthful and murder respectable, and to give an appearance of solidity to pure wind (ibid).

ORWELL'S LOATHING OF TOTALITARIANISM

This is the theme which mattered most to Orwell; it stems from his absolute loathing of 'totalitarianism' – a catch-all phrase which describes the corrupt truth-denying philosophy that unified fascism and communism in the twentieth century. Hannah Arendt, the political theorist who after observing Eichmann's trial coined the phrase 'the banality of evil', wrote:

Whenever totalitarianism possesses absolute control, it replaces propaganda with indoctrination and uses violence not so much to frighten people … as to realize constantly its ideological doctrines and its practical lies. Totalitarianism will not be satisfied to assert, in the face of contrary facts, that unemployment does not exist; it will abolish unemployment benefits as part of its propaganda. … Or when, to take another instance, Stalin decided to rewrite the history of the Russian Revolution, the propaganda of his new version consisted of destroying, together with the older books and documents, their authors and readers (Arendt 1975: 341-342).

Orwell echoes this idea when he writes in his essay 'Looking back on the Spanish war':

> Nazi theory indeed specifically denies that such a thing as 'the truth' exists. .. If the Leader says of such and such an event, 'It never happened' – well, it never happened. If he says that two and two are five – well, two and two are five (Orwell 1980 [1942]: 601).

And this brings us back to *Nineteen Eighty-Four*: a world in which Winston Smith's torturer O'Brien explains that two and two do, in fact, make five; where the Ministry of Truth generates lies; where news is faked and history is falsified and a permanent state of war exists for no reason other than to sustain the totalitarian regimes that control the planet. The essence of totalitarianism is that it wants to control *everything*. Hearts, minds, souls, reality itself. It is more than despotism. It is the enemy of everything good and true. Hitler and Stalin were both totalitarians. Mao's regime in China too was founded on the principle that the people's minds and souls could be *controlled*. And all three dictators shared a belief that the empirical and hypothesis-testing paradigm that is the essence of the scientific enterprise could be discarded at their own personal whim. Millions died in Russia and China because of this delusion. In Russia, the cult of Lysenkoism attempted to usurp the scientific discipline of genetics; and in consequence, the fields were seeded with graves, by the million.

Orwell, in *Nineteen Eighty-Four* and in much of his political writings, waged a ceaseless war against totalitarian nonsense with all the skill, rhetoric and scorn at his disposal – which was considerable. *Nineteen Eighty-Four* is all about the manipulation of reality that is emblematic of the totalitarian project. In the final stages of the novel, O'Brien tells Winston Smith:

> You believe that reality is something objective, external, existing in its own right. You also believe that the nature of reality is self-evident. When you delude yourself into thinking that you see something, you assume that everyone else sees the same thing as you. But I tell you, Winston, that reality is not external. Reality exists in the human mind, and nowhere else. Not in the individual mind, which can make mistakes, and in any case soon perishes: only in the mind of the Party, which is collective and immortal. Whatever the Party holds to be the truth, is truth (Orwell 1976 [1949]: 886).

This directly reflects Stalin's political strategy, as recounted by Orwell in his essay 'Inside the Whale':

> Every time Stalin swaps partners, 'Marxism' has to be hammered into a new shape. This entails sudden and violent changes of 'line', purges, denunciations, systematic destruction of party literature, etc. ... Every Communist is in fact liable at any moment to have to alter his most fundamental convictions, or leave the party. The unquestionable dogma of Monday may become the damnable heresy of Tuesday, and so on (Orwell 1980 [1940b]: 508).

THE LANGUAGE OF NEWSPEAK

This is what Stalin believed. And so all totalitarians believe. They are convinced that to say something is so, will make it so. It is an insane delusion. For if you believe that two and two make five then your aeroplanes will fall out of the sky and your machines will explode and your climate will, destructively, change. That way madness lies. Or, more accurately in our tumultuous times, *this* way madness lies. And language is at the heart of it. Language can be the conduit for truth, or it can be the embodiment of lies. And this is the insight which Orwell captured with his invented language of Newspeak. A language that includes words like *blackwhite* with its two mutually contradictory meanings. Applied to an opponent, it means the habit of impudently claiming that black is white, in contradiction of the plain facts. Applied to a Party member, it means a loyal willingness to say that black is white when Party discipline demands this. But it means also the ability to *believe* that black is white.

Another chilling word is *thoughtcrime* – an occurrence or instance of controversial or socially unacceptable thoughts. In Orwell's Newspeak, an *unperson* is a person who has been 'abolished'; who has not only been killed by the state, but effectively erased from existence. And *doublethink* is the act of holding two contradictory beliefs in one's mind simultaneously, and accepting both of them. Newspeak, and its defining principle of *doublethink*, constitute the purest form of banal rhetoric. Together, they create a prison of the mind, in which the prisoner does not even realise there is a world outside the bars.

REFERENCES

Arendt, Hannah (1975) *The Origins of Totalitarianism,* San Diego: Harvest Books

Bergman, Ronen (2008) *The Secret War with Iran: The 30-Year Covert Struggle for Control of a 'Rogue' State*, Oxford: One World

Churchill, Winston (1940) 'We shall fight them on the beaches', speech to parliament, June. Available online at http://audio.theguardian.tv/sys-audio/Guardian/audio/2007/04/20/Churchill.mp3

Orwell, George (1980 [1940a]) Charles Dickens, *George Orwell*, London: Secker and Warburg pp 443-477

PHILIP PALMER

Orwell, George (1980 [1940b]) Inside the Whale, *George Orwell*, London: Secker and Warburg pp 494-518

Orwell, George (1980 [1942]) Looking back on the Spanish Civil War, *George Orwell*, London: Secker and Warburg pp 595-607

Orwell, George (1980 [1946]) Politics and the English language, *George Orwell*, London: Secker and Warburg pp 735-743

Orwell, George (1976 [1949]) *Nineteen Eighty-Four*, *George Orwell*, London: Secker and Warburg pp 741-925

NOTE ON THE CONTRIBUTOR

Philip Palmer is a Senior Lecturer at Goldsmiths, convening and teaching courses in creative writing and screenwriting. He is also a novelist, screenwriter, television writer and radio dramatist. He has written five SF novels for Orbit Books: *Debatable Space, Version 43, Red Claw, Hell Ship* and *Artemis*. And his new urban fantasy/crime novel *Hell on Earth* was published in 2017 under the Hellbooks imprint. Over twenty years he has written thrillers, crime dramas, historical dramas, drama docs and science fiction and fantasy stories. His numerous radio credits include two series of the Cold War cop drama *Keeping the Wolf Out* starring Leo Bill and Clare Corbett, nominated in 2016 for the BBC Audio Awards; the historical thriller *The King's Coiner*, starring Ian McDiarmid; two SF dramas for BBC radio, *Invasion* and *Dark Souls*; and *The Faerie Queene* starring Simon Russell Beale. He is founder of Afan Films and creative director of IFL and has two movie projects at development/financing stage.

ARTICLE

A Short History of Hate

SEAN CUBITT

This article analyses how the theme of hate depicted in Orwell's dystopian novel Nineteen Eighty-Four *has been transformed in representations – from the BBC's live television production by Nigel Kneale and Rudolf Cartier, in 1954, to Ridley Scott's commercial for Apple computers in 1984. It goes on to consider the significance of artist Terry Flaxton's video that was shot separately on the set and the meanings to be drawn from the interviews with east London skinheads who took part in the group-hate scene. The article argues that Orwell's dystopian vision offers an inspiration for understanding how the nature of hate has changed from individual performance in community assemblies and mass rallies to what might be defined as an 'aggregation of behaviours'. The hate of today is not to be found on television, in advertising campaigns or festival documentaries but in Twitter storms and social media bullying.*

Keywords: capitalism, hate, individualism, neoliberalism, *Nineteen Eighty-Four*, Orwell

> The horrible thing about the Two Minutes Hate was not that one was obliged to play a part but, on the contrary, that it was impossible to avoid joining in (Orwell 1998 [1949]: 16).

INTRODUCTION

In 1984, Apple Computers launched the Mac with an advertisement screened at the half-time break in the Super Bowl, traditionally the most-watched and most expensive commercial break in US broadcasting. The commercial was shot by the Hollywood director Ridley Scott on the theme 'Why 1984 won't be like *1984*', using visual motifs from Orwell's novel (for an analysis of the commercial circumstances and production thinking, see Chapter 5 of Friedman 2005). Hired to shoot the making-of a documentary for this expensive production, Terry Flaxton created an artist's video from the footage shot on set, including disturbing interviews with the East End skinheads hired as extras for the group-hate sequence. Viewed alongside the BBC's 1954 *Sunday Night Theatre* production, written by Nigel Kneale and directed by Rudolf Cartier (who also teamed up for three series of *Quatermass*, a celebrated BBC science fiction series first broadcast in 1953), Scott's commercial and Flaxton's meta-documentary can help us explore how hatred has evolved – through the experiences of colonialism and conflict, as reflected on by Orwell during his sojourn on the remote Scottish island of Jura between 1947 and 1948, and the Cold War to Thatcher's Britain and beyond. Precisely because it is not the last word on the matter, Orwell's *mythos* has retained the power to anatomise hatred into the present century.

ORWELL AND THE COLD WAR

Recruiting Orwell for the ideological flank of the Cold War was not difficult: it was always easy to ascribe Big Brother's characteristic to the enemy. This straightforwardly ideological reading has a degree of truth but is unsatisfying. A richer reading becomes possible if we place his vision of Britain as Airstrip One with Horkheimer and Adorno's (1973) nearly contemporaneous theory of the 'administered society' and Arendt's (1958) slightly later 'totalitarianism'. Both reckon Hitler's nazism as only an extreme form of a more pervasive triumph: that of instrumental rationality whose outlines the nazis fleshed out from the bureaucratic system and the accompanying urban anxieties whose outlines had been pencilled by Weber (1946) and Simmel (1950).

Alternatively, from today's perspective, if we restrict our understanding of *Nineteen Eighty-Four* to a parable about Stalinism or see it as a critique of the emergent welfare state bureaucracy and the post-war consensus, we reduce it to a period piece and are left without an explanation for its lasting power as an evocation of oppression and resistance. This is by no means to decry the value of historical scholarship around Orwell's life and his intellectual and political formation: his experience of colonialism in Burma and with the down-and-outs in Paris and London and his state of mind while he was seriously ill on Jura between 1947 and 1948. There may well be something of the memories of Eton, the discipline of the colonial policeman and the anarchism of POUM (the Spanish militia alongside whom he fought during the Spanish civil war) which all helped form Orwell the journalist, the extraordinary interpreter of his own time.

Orwell's novels are unimaginable without taking into account his career in journalism. *Nineteen Eighty-Four* extends beyond its own time paradoxically because it captures the immediate post-war mood so profoundly. The current rhetoric about 'alternative facts' and the pressing issue of post-truth journalism can both be usefully understood in the context of Orwell's notion of newspeak: the language of the totalitarian state of Oceania, constantly at war with either Eurasia or Eastasia. One of Orwell's enduring images is of his anti-hero Winston Smith hiding from the all-seeing telescreen to practise the forbidden and write his diary. Indeed, to what extent do the hysterical propaganda broadcasts of Goebbels, Lord Haw Haw and Ezra Pound anticipate the Two Minutes Hate?

ORWELL'S MEDIA THEORY

In Airstrip One, television is a two-way medium – as it had been imagined in pre-war films from Maurice Elvey's 1927 silent *High Treason* to the W. C. Fields vehicle *International House* (1933). Orwell makes the two-way communication the state's gateway into the private lives of its citizens. Today, even though state surveillance remains a major force (see for example Harding 2014), an equal if not greater danger of surveillance media comes from the corporate sector, not the state (Elmer 2004, Jeffreys-Jones 2017). When Orwell wrote in the middle of the last century, the state was the dominant instrument of exploitation, oppression and terror. Today that role has been taken over by the market and private businesses. Nonetheless, Orwell was right to stress that the mobilisation of hate is a core function of media and equally that the media do not *originate* hate. Orwell, instead, insists that media *organise* hate. In the novel, as in many of its screen interpretations, the representation of the Two Minutes Hate is terrifying. But hate is not confined to that event – it still lies in Winston's tortured soul that Orwell anatomises, most chillingly in his fantasy of raping and wanting to kill Julia.

In the novel, Orwell emphasises the power of the image, of montage and proto-subliminal cross fades of Emmanuel Goldstein (the Enemy No. 1) with the image of a sheep and then a soldier attacking. Cartier's staging on the contrary emphasises the verbal, especially the slogans (War is peace, Freedom is slavery, Ignorance is strength) that Orwell dwelt on whose intrinsic meaninglessness disappears under their repetition. Winston writing obsessively 'Down with Big Brother' in his diary is authentic because it is the physical expression of his inmost thought. Its opposite is the inauthentic and disembodied transmission of the Ingsoc propaganda constantly beamed into his cabbage-smelling flat. The Two Minutes Hate of the BBC dramatisation is conducted in a dim room illuminated only by the telescreen, with a handful of co-workers on rows of unfixed, utility chairs. The Nigel Kneale/Rudolph Cartier BBC adaptation captures all the drabness of post-war austerity Britain and the claustrophobia of small communities where everyone watches everyone else – a surveillance culture all the more threatening because of its familiarity and domestication.

HATE FROM COMMUNITY TO MASS

True to Orwell, Cartier's cross cut from the mounting cries of hatred to the soldier firing into the telescreen lens makes its point: television has the power to ignite hate. Yet it is also clear that this hatred is not new. Both novel and script emphasise that the hate is already there, waiting for the sanction that will allow it to erupt;

even to the point that Winston can always direct his hatred. To play on a truism of media theory, media cannot tell us what to think but they do instruct us on how to think.

The hate we witness in both novel and BBC adaptation belongs to what Tönnies (1955), one of the founding fathers of sociology, referred to as *Gemeinschaft*: the community of shared traditions and values that he feared had disappeared in the urbanisations of the late 19th century. It was just such a community that was rediscovered by Orwell's contemporaries: the mid-century anthropology of Mass Observation (1943), the autobiographical writings of Richard Hoggart (1957), the working class histories of communists such as E. P. Thompson (1963) and a founding moment of media theory in Raymond Williams (1958; see also Williams 1971). Hannah Arendt (1965), in the wake of the Eichmann trial, would coin exactly the term for this mode of hate born of proximity, common values and self-surveillance: the banality of evil. The hate is communal, not mass: that is why it was impossible not to join in – in 1948 or 1954.

Thirty years later, with Churchill replaced as PM by Thatcher, hate had changed shape. Tönnies' communal *Gemeinschaft* gives way to *Gesellschaft:* the mass society. Historian and political philosopher Michel Foucault (2000) offers a subtle distinction between two forms of mass society; disciplinary societies – which encourage each member to internalise its rules through perpetual fear of observation – and biopolitical societies in which human life processes are managed under regimes of authority over knowledge, power and the processes of subjectivity. The difference is visible in the change from omnipresent enforcement of norms by constant pressure to conform in the 1954 version to the mass spectacle of Michael Radford's *1984* feature film adaptation. In many respects, Radford's account of the Two Minutes Hate – despite being much closer to the letter of the novel – is misleading in its totalitarian setting, both in relation to Orwell's enclosed community of haters and in relation to Thatcher's Britain which prioritised the rolling back of the state.

Also in 1984, Ridley Scott (who had sprung to prominence with the 1982 release of his dystopian *Blade Runner*) was commissioned to direct an advertisement to accompany the release of the Apple Mac personal computer. The ad would be aired in a break in the Super Bowl, then the most expensive airtime on American TV. The ad is listed as one of the top commercials of all time and regarded as a watershed in the industry. As a vast crowd of shaven-headed proles moan in unison, a rainbow-dressed woman races into the arena, hurling a hammer into the totalitarian screen to smash it. The tagline – 'Why 1984 won't be like *1984*' – promoted the myth of Apple's 'brave little creative culture' smashing the tyranny of IBM and Microsoft and helped define its brand for decades to come. In the advert, the neoliberal ethos of Radford's film meets the new paradigm of creative industries, soon to be institutionalised in Silicon Fen (the region around Cambridge housing a large cluster of high-tech businesses) and Old Street's Silicon Roundabout (the home of numerous web companies in East London). In 1984, neither the revolution nor even the entrepreneurial individual would smash the state: rather it was the brand.

HATE AND INDIVIDUALISM

But we have not yet arrived at the most telling version of *1984* in 1984. Hired to shoot the making-of the film by agency Chiat/Day, cinematographer and video artist Terry Flaxton recorded interviews with the East End skinheads hired as extras for Scott's shoot. In *Prisoners,* the video he made from this material, Flaxton catches the underlying hatred of the skinheads in the looped comment: 'We want what we want.' This is not the mass-orchestrated hate of the advertisement (or Radford's film) but the terrible truth of the street hatred encouraged by Thatcher's individualist, anti-communitarian drive towards a property-owning democracy. Here the unleashing of anti-state energies turns towards blaming the victims of emergent neo-liberalism: the neighbourhood poor always easier to blame than the invisible and anonymous beneficiaries of Thatcherite tax breaks and deregulation.

Flaxton has mixed sympathies: the skinheads' blunt embrace of offensive language and indecent attitudes is the decaying refusenik attitude of a community under siege. Ernesto Laclau (2005) argues that populist movements are neither outbursts of blind rage nor symptoms of demagoguery but expressions of genuine needs that the existing polity fails or refuses to meet. It is these real needs that the demagogue articulates in political movements that are both destructive howls of collective wrath and fierce critiques of entrenched power. At the same time, the anarchy of skinhead hate is significantly (mis)guided into racism and gendered expletives. This hyper-masculine hatred arose in response to Thatcher's deliberate attack on the working class and the creation of mass unemployment.

David Widgery's 1986 book tracing the history of Rock Against Racism begins with a chilling description of the wounds received by a middle aged Asian man at the hands of a National Front mob. This street hate is real – so very different from the mythical, Nuremberg-like scenes in Radford and Scott's evocations of the Two Minutes Hate. Thatcherism had already begun those surgical interventions that would end the post-war consensus and attack the welfare state on the basis of the neo-Darwinian individualist ideology of neo-liberalism. This enforced individualist ethos structures the uniformity of dress and haircut, the homosociality, and the inchoate racist and sexist rage of these young working class men: ironically the first to suffer from both the wreckage of welfare state solidarity and the brutal assertion of individualism.

Scott imagined the Two Minutes Hate as a Roman spectacle, a spectacle of imperial might over the souls of the slaves of the kind revived by Mussolini and Hitler in the 1930s and discredited by their defeat. Scott's version is, therefore, both anachronistic and an easy target. Curiously, given Orwell's description of the event which both men and women attend (followed by Cartier and with even greater fidelity by Radford), Scott's imperial spectacle of a regimented mass is also entirely male (leaving both the heroine and the product to be cast as feminine). In Foucault's world, as in Orwell's, each citizen internalises the demands of authority and, as a result, ubiquitous surveillance becomes commonplace and internalised as *self*-surveillance. Among Flaxton's skinheads, a new form of hate is emerging, appropriate to what Foucault would call biopolitics: the management of populations otherwise left by the state to their own devices.

THE FUTURE OF HATE

If we look today for the Two Minutes Hate, we do not find it on television, advertising nor even in documentary. It persists on talk radio, a few cable TV channels and in the overtly right-wing press and broadcast television channels. But hate is at its most unavoidable in Twitter storms and macho, social media bullying. It reflects both nostalgia for the myth of individualism 'when a man could stand four square, putting his body on the line' and a new nostalgia for a mythic masculinity acted out by shock jocks and Fleet Street columnists looking back to the residual authenticity of the skins, even though that was itself a nostalgic recreation of some earlier, more *Gemeinschaftlich* social cohesion. Contemporary hate no longer places each man's body at risk. It is conducted at a distance, on keypads and monitors, minimal physical gestures of fingers and eyes that risk no physical retaliation. Even the men involved in mass shootings or suicide bombings are denied the scars to prove their manliness because no body is left. The body now is a remnant. It is disposable, no longer wagered as Pascal wagered his soul on the existence of God.

Contemporary hate is no longer mass performance of allegiance, communal performance of consolidated norms or individuated performance of a lost authenticity. The desperate 'look at me look at me' plea of the right-wing Breitbart News Network and Trumpism is nostalgic for a lost masculinity. As the nuclear family, heir to the communal extended kinship group, collapsed under the pressures of consumerism in the 1960s, so the individual, cursed with the burdens of responsibility under neoliberalism, is beginning to fall apart – leading to the epidemics of mental illness we are now witnessing. The obligations to consume and communicate have superseded older eras of productive and service economies (see, among others, Brown 2015, Dean 2009 and Harvey 2010). Pursuing the logic of the division of labour into the digital age, the search engines, social media platforms, news aggregators and microblogs that dominate the emergent economy collect, collate, curate and commercialise micro-gestures on touchscreens, GPS trackers and health-monitoring apps. The individual disappears in this cloud of data. What is of interest is no longer the individual but behaviours.

This is no surprise to data scientists, bemused at the idea that the self has even a residual part in this network of mass connectivity. Like the extended and nuclear families, the individual is now a residue of older social organisations: an appendix left behind by evolution. Hate today does not look like the assembled workmates of 1954, and certainly not the mass rally of *Nineteen Eighty-Four*. Even when the Trump and Le Pen rallies (in France) seek to capture today's hatred, they do so perpetually in nostalgic mode, mixing the demands for an authoritarian emperor, a normative community and savage individualism simultaneously.

In place of mass, community or individual hatred, today it is transformed into an aggregation of behaviours. The 'I' that tweets is a person, good or bad, but they are insignificant in the eyes of the databases that count and account for interactions. Only the hateful tweet, the gesture of hatred, a moment of behaviour, counts. The next tweet from the same account may be about rabbits or cooking tips. This is not because brutality is psychologically twinned with sentimentality. Today, the flick of two fingers, the cuddling of bunnies and the hints on baking do not add up to a whole: they are discrete behaviours linked by 'likes' and 'shares' to other similar behaviours into nodes formed not of individuals or communities but effervescent trends.

CONCLUSION

Hate, Orwell teaches us, is an instrument of rule that works because it reaches into the unhappy soul and invites it to spit out its bile. Winston can even hate Big Brother, but he has no choice about hate itself. In Orwell's novel, hate is compulsory and compulsorily public, while love must be kept secret. The inference is that in a healthy world, love is public while hate is ashamed of itself. Hate in that case is the most intimate of emotions.

In this brief history of hate, for all its changing operations, Orwell's analysis still holds. True power lies not in directing the bile but in permitting, encouraging, demanding it. In the face of the emergent mass society, Orwell promoted the notion of the free individual. Like Winston's discovery that he can hate Big Brother, and paralleling Fanon's anti-colonial plea for hatred as a necessary tool of liberation (1961), we may still need to mobilise hate in some new way to explode once more the shackles of our contemporary corporate Big Brother in order to discover some future form of love.

ACKNOWLEDGEMENT

The author is grateful to Professor John Hill and the AHRC History of Forgotten Television Drama in the UK research project for access to the Cartier/Kneale adaptation and to Terry Flaxton for permission to use stills from *Prisoners* in his Goldsmiths presentation.

REFERENCES

Arendt, Hannah (1958) *The Origins of Totalitarianism*, Cleveland: The World Publishing Company, second edition

Arendt, Hannah (1965) *Eichmann in Jerusalem: A Report on the Banality of Evil*, Harmondsworth: Penguin, revised edition

Brown, Wendy (2015) *Undoing the Demos: Neoliberalism's Stealth Revolution*, New York: Zone Books

Dean, Jodi (2009) *Democracy and Other Neoliberal Fantasies: Communicative Capitalism and Left Politics,* Durham NC: Duke University Press

Elmer, Greg (2004) *Profiling Machines: Mapping the Personal Information Economy*, Cambridge MA: MIT Press

Fanon, Frantz (1961) *The Wretched of the Earth*, London: Penguin

Foucault, Michel (2000) Governmentality, Faubion, James D. (ed.) *Power: Essential Works of Foucault 1954-1984*, Vol. 3 (trans. by Hurley, Robert) London: Penguin pp 201-222

Friedman, Ted (2005). *Electric Dreams: Computers in American Culture*, New York: New York University Press

Harding, Luke (2014) *The Snowden Files: The Inside Story of the World's Most Wanted Man,* New York: Vintage Books

Harvey, David (2010) *The Enigma of Capital and the Crises of Capitalism*, Oxford: Oxford University Press

Hoggart, Richard (1957) *The Uses of Literacy: Aspects of Working Class Life*, London: Chatto and Windus.

Horkheimer, Max and Adorno, Theodor (1973) *The Dialectic of Enlightenment* (trans by Cumming, John), London: Allen Lane

Jeffreys-Jones, Rhodri (2017) *We Know All About You: The Story of Surveillance in Britain and America*, Oxford: Oxford University Press

Mass-Observation (1943) *The Pub and the People,* London: Gollancz

Orwell, George, (1998 [1949]) *Nineteen Eighty-Four: The Complete Works of George Orwell, Vol. 9*, London: Secker & Warburg

Simmel, Georg (1950) The metropolis and mental life, Wolff, Kurt H. (ed.) *The Sociology of Georg Simmel*, New York: The Free Press pp 409-424

Thompson, E. P. (1963) *The Making of the English Working Class*, London: Gollancz

Tönnies, Ferdinand (1955) *Community and Association (Gemeinschaft und Gesellschaft)*, London: Routledge & Kegan Paul

Weber, Max (1946) Bureaucracy, Gerth, H. H. and Mills, C. Wright (eds and trans) *From Max Weber: Essays in Sociology*, New York: Oxford University Press pp 196-244

Widgery, David (1986) *Beating Time: Riot 'n' Race 'n' Rock 'n' Roll*, London: Tiger Stripe Books

Williams, Raymond (1958) *Culture and Society 1780-1950*, Harmondsworth: Penguin

Williams, Raymond (1971) *Orwell*, Glasgow: Fontana

NOTE ON THE CONTRIBUTOR

Sean Cubitt is Professor of Film and Television at Goldsmiths, University of London, and Honorary Professorial Fellow of the University of Melbourne. His publications include *The Cinema Effect*, *The Practice of Light*: *Genealogies of Visual Media* and *Finite Media*: *Environmental Implications of Digital Technology*. Series editor for Leonardo Books at MIT Press, his current research is on political aesthetics, media technologies, media art history and ecocriticism.

ARTICLE

ARTICLE

Orwell, the Labour Party and the Attlee Government

JOHN NEWSINGER

John Newsinger examines Orwell's complex and ever-shifting attitudes to the Independent Labour Party and then the Labour Party from the mid-1930s until his death in 1950.

Throughout the 1930s and into the early 1940s, George Orwell had a very low estimation of the Labour Party. This was obviously in response to its performance in office in 1929-31, but it was not just that. The conception of democratic socialism that Orwell came to embrace in the course of the 1930s had very little in common with Labourism. Socialism, for Orwell, meant a classless society where the ruling class had been altogether dispossessed, deprived of their wealth, power and status, rather than one where they had, however reluctantly, acquiesced in some amelioration of the condition of the working class and agreed to allow suitable trade union leaders and Labour politicians to enter the House of Lords. Moreover, the fate of the Spanish revolution during the late 1930s convinced him that the ruling class would inevitably resist its dispossession and that this resistance would have to be put down by however much force was necessary. This obviously had little in common with British Labourism with its history of accommodation, compromise and betrayal.

Even before he went to Spain, in December 1936, he found the Independent Labour Party (ILP) that had broken away from the Labour Party after the MacDonald debacle in 1931 to be the most congenial political home. He was in sympathy with its anti-imperialism, its anti-Stalinism and its commitment – not to piecemeal reform but to fundamental root-and-branch change. At this time, Orwell rejected what he saw as the Bolshevik model of revolution: of the working class taking power through armed insurrection. This model was inappropriate in a country like Britain, regardless of debates about how the Russian revolution had turned out. Instead, he looked to the growth of a powerful mass movement based on the trade union rank and file that would elect an ILP-led majority to the Commons. This majority would proceed to the immediate dispossession of the ruling class, not reform, but revolution. He did not expect the British ruling class to respond to this with the ferocity of the Spanish so that a full-scale civil war was most unlikely, but there would be sabotage and resistance. The mass movement that had carried the ILP to power would put this opposition down, shooting people if necessary, and it would be London not Barcelona that swirled with red flags as the British working class established itself in power, putting up barricades and taking over the factories. His main criticism of the ILP at this time was that they did not recognise the urgent need to win over white collar workers and the professional classes to the socialist cause.

Orwell joined the ILP on his return from fighting in Spain. On 24 June 1938, the ILP paper, the *New Leader*, published his 'Why I Join the ILP'. The essential reason was that 'the ILP is the only British party … which aims at anything I should regard as Socialism'. To be fair, in the next paragraph, he insisted that this did 'not mean that I have lost all faith in the Labour Party', indeed, he hoped that Labour would 'win a clear majority in the next General Election'. Nevertheless, one had to remember the Labour Party's history and its readiness 'to fling every principle overboard'. The ILP, he felt, would never, in any circumstances, 'compromise their Socialist principles'. And, of course, he had fought alongside ILP members and the neo-Trotskyite POUM militia in Spain where, while he did not agree with every detail of POUM and ILP policy, 'the general course of events has borne it out' (*CWGO* 11: 168).[1]

He shared the ILP's attitude to the Stalinists' crushing of the revolutionary left in Spain, something that they argued in their press and in publications such as Fenner Brockway's hard-hitting pamphlet, *The Truth about Barcelona* (1937). Here he celebrated the workers' takeover of 'their factories and workshops, of the railways and trams, of the telephone service and the broadcasting station, of the hotels, the cinemas and the theatres'. All this was championed and defended by the POUM which made it the Stalinists prime target when they set about rolling the revolution back. As Brockway bluntly put it:

> In Barcelona in 1937 the POUM fulfilled the historic role which the Bolsheviks fulfilled in Moscow in 1917. The Communists took the part of the Mensheviks. Just as the Bolsheviks were charged with being German agents, so the POUM is now charged, ironically enough by the Communists with being Fascist agents.

Brockway looked forward to the victory of the Spanish workers: 'a triumph which will not only shatter Fascism, but lay the foundations of the new Workers' State of Socialism' (Brockway 1937: 3-4, 14).

According to Orwell, Brockway's pamphlet 'so far as my own knowledge goes is entirely accurate'(*CWGO* 11: 55). In his important book, *Workers' Front,* published by Secker and Warburg in 1938,

ARTICLE

JOHN NEWSINGER

Brockway revisited communist conduct in Spain, challenged the politics of the Popular Front, proclaiming the ILP a 'Revolutionary Socialist' party and calling for the formation of a 'Workers' Front'. While it was prepared to make use of parliament, the ILP, he made clear, 'does not accept the Labour Party view that the transition to Socialism can be made through the apparatus of the Capitalist State' and rejected 'the Labour Party's programme of the gradual transformation of Capitalism to Socialism'. And he also made clear that the ILP rejected the Labour Party's policy of nationalising 'leading industries, instead of socialising them out and out'. He went on to savage the 1929-31 Labour government for its policy regarding India, refusing either to 'extend self-government to India' or 'release Indian political prisoners'. It consequently had to repress a mass civil disobedience movement and became 'responsible for imprisoning 60,000 Indians' (Brockway 1938: 85-86, 216, 254). Indeed, the situation was actually worse than Brockway described, involving shootings, hangings and public floggings as well as mass imprisonment. Orwell, reviewed the book in February 1938 in the *New English Weekly*, taking the opportunity to condemn 'the nauseous spectacle of bishops, Communists, cocoa-magnates, publishers, duchesses and Labour MPs marching arm in arm to the tune of "Rule Britannia"' (*CWGO* 11: 124). It is interesting that the ILP was the only political party that Orwell ever joined.

REVOLUTIONARY PATRIOTISM

In the event, Orwell was to break with the ILP over the Second World War. It maintained its opposition whereas he performed a dramatic turnaround. By 1940, however, he was arguing that only a socialist revolution would enable Britain to defeat the Nazis. He did not see the Labour Party as the vehicle of this revolution. In many respects, he remained true to the programme of the ILP with the exception of its anti-war stance. In February 1941, he published an article, 'Fascism and Democracy' in *Left News*. Here, he made the point that 'there is no certainty that the rule of a privileged class can ever be broken by purely democratic means'. In the unlikely event of a Labour government trying 'to establish socialism by Act of Parliament ... the monied classes would rebel. ... There is no strong reason for thinking that any really fundamental change can ever be achieved peacefully'. And as for the Labour Party: 'Whatever programmes the Labour Party may issue, it has been difficult for ten years past to believe that its leaders expected or even wished to see any fundamental change in their lifetime.' Instead, he hoped for the emergence of a 'real English socialist movement ... both revolutionary and democratic. It will aim at the most fundamental changes and be perfectly willing to use violence if necessary' (*CWGO* 12: 377, 380, 381).

Orwell repeated his dismissal of the Labour Party in his short book, *The Lion and the Unicorn*, one of the Searchlight series that was published by Secker and Warburg in February 1941. Here, he conceded that in Britain 'there is only one Socialist party that has ever seriously mattered, the Labour Party' but that its subordination to the trade unions meant that 'all through the critical years it was directly interested in the prosperity of British capitalism' and 'in the maintenance of the British Empire'. And anyway, 'all the key points', by which he meant the military, the civil service, the judiciary, the diplomatic corps and intelligence services, 'were in the hands of its enemies'. The consequence of this was that once in power, 'the same dilemma would always have faced it: carry out your promises, and risk revolt, or continue with the same policy as the Conservatives, and stop talking about Socialism'. The certainty of upper class resistance to fundamental change was a recurring theme of Orwell's writing that has not received enough notice. Moreover, he actually doubted whether from 1935 on they even 'had any wish to take office. They had degenerated into a Permanent Opposition'. All the Labour Party stood for was 'a timid reformism' with its leaders' ambitions limited to 'drawing their salaries and periodically swapping jobs with the Conservatives'. Indeed, 'Labour Party politics had become a variant of Conservatism' (*CWGO* 12: 418-419, 420-421).

One last point worth noting here is Orwell's response to the much-fêted Beveridge report, of November 1942, on social security, the keystone of Labour's post-war welfare state. As far as he was concerned, all it amounted to was a 'very modest measure of reform' (*CWGO* 14: 292). However much many Conservatives might object to this cosseting of the working class, it never posed any threat to the wealth and power of the rich. To be blunt, if it had the Attlee government would never have implemented it.

TRIBUNE AND THE LABOUR PARTY

Orwell's hopes for the emergence of a new socialist movement that would sweep away the old ruling class and put in place a system of democratic socialism, something that he believed essential for the defeat of Nazism, were, as he admitted, mistaken. The ruling class remained securely in place and yet the war was not lost. It was in these circumstance that he went to work in November 1943 for the left-Labour weekly newspaper, *Tribune*, recognising, however reluctantly, that the Labour Party was the only serious alternative to the Conservatives. He did not actually join the Labour Party though, and *Tribune* was, at that time, very much an opposition newspaper: critical, often extremely critical, of the Churchill Coalition government which Labour had joined. Even so, it is important to remember that most of his discussion of British politics was not written for the pages of *Tribune*, but for the far-left US magazine, *Partisan Review*.[2] There was no British equivalent of *Partisan Review*. If there had been, Orwell would certainly have written for it and his commitment to British Labourism at this time would be recognised as far more equivocal than it generally is. As well as *Tribune*, he would have been regularly writing for a British neo-Trotskyist magazine that was openly critical of the British Labour tradition.

Nevertheless, his association through *Tribune* with politicians such as Aneurin Bevan does seem to have convinced him that there was a possibility that a future Labour government might actually take on the British ruling class. Orwell gave up his position as literary editor on the journal in February 1945 (to become a war correspondent for the *Observer* and *Manchester Evening News*) and did not return as a columnist until October after Labour had been elected to power. He did not expect Labour to win the July 1945 general election but the appointment of the likes of Bevan to the government raised his hopes that a real challenge to the ruling class was in the offing. His hopes in this respect were as wildly over-optimistic as his wartime hopes of revolution had been.

Writing in *Partisan Review*, he outlined to his American readers what see saw as the significance of Labour's victory. Many people had voted Labour for 'family allowances, higher old age pensions, houses with bathrooms etc' rather than for socialism. Certainly, the victory should not be taken as an indication 'that Britain is on the verge of revolution'. Indeed, he thought there was less of a revolutionary mood in the country than there had been in 1940. As far as he could see, of the votes cast for Labour only 'at most 50 per cent could be considered as outright votes for Socialism'. The remainder were for ameliorative welfare measures. What he hoped was that the Labour government would set about re-educating public opinion, although he admitted that this 'to a large extent means fighting against its own past propaganda'. He told his readers how they could judge whether the government actually meant business or not (this was written in the middle of August 1945). It would 'nationalise land, coal mines, railways, public utilities and banks', offer 'India immediate Dominium Status (this is a minimum)' and begin a purge of 'the bureaucracy, the army, the Diplomatic Service etc., so thoroughly as to forestall sabotage from the right'. He expected an immediate clash with the House of Lords. If this didn't happen, 'it is a good bet that no really radical economic change is intended'.

Orwell hoped the Labour government would launch an immediate attack on the ruling class and in the process 're-educate' the working class as he put it. When he wrote of nationalisation, he was not thinking of the state taking over bankrupt industries and paying extremely generous compensation. He was advocating outright confiscation and quite correctly he believed that this would provoke resistance which would have to be put down. In many respects what he was advocating was that the Labour government would implement the pre-war ILP programme. Whether it would or not was another matter. As he put it: 'Heaven knows whether the government has any serious intention of introducing Socialism, but if it has, I don't see what there is to stop it' (*CWGO* 17: 246, 249).

Tosco Fyvel had replaced Orwell as literary editor of *Tribune* and he has recalled how, when Orwell proposed once again writing for the newspaper, he had wanted to attack its moderation. He wanted to argue in *Tribune*'s pages that 'the new Labour government must make its first Socialist task to abolish all titles, the House of Lords and the Public Schools' (Fyvel 1971: 115). There was, of course, absolutely no chance whatsoever that this would happen. Not only was Prime Minister Attlee a staunch public school man, keen to have as many former public school boys in his Labour government as possible, but he was also a strong believer in the efficacy of the House of Lords. A recent biography of Attlee (that won the Orwell Prize no less) was entitled *Citizen Clem* (Bew 2016), whereas a more appropriate title given Attlee's proclivities would have been Viscount Clem. Attlee and the rest of his government were committed not to the emancipation of the working class but to its improvement. They believed that the situation of the working class should be improved both as a good thing in itself but also because this would make Britain stronger. Moreover, this Britain was very much a great power Britain, an imperial Britain. They certainly had no intention of throwing down a challenge to the ruling class.

As far as Orwell was concerned, the immediate abolition of the public schools and of the House of Lords, two great bastions of privilege, would have posed a direct threat to the power and position of the ruling class. But they would have certainly have resisted – opening the way for a popular radicalisation which could have carried the country to socialism. For Orwell, socialism still meant a classless society where the rich had been expropriated and altogether abolished, rather than a society where the working class remained exactly where they were in the class system but with an amelioration in their living conditions.

There is no doubt that Orwell's relations with *Tribune* cooled once Labour was in power. In December 1947, he complained to his friend Julian Symons that *Tribune* was getting 'worse and worse'. The paper looked 'fearfully left' but in the end always came down 'on the side of the government whenever there is a major issue'. He blamed this on the pernicious influence that Richard Crossman MP exercised over Michael Foot and Tosco Fyvel (*CWGO* 19: 250). These feelings were reciprocated with Foot remembering Orwell as becoming 'detached from if not hostile to his old *Tribune* associations'. He put this down to Orwell feeling they were not hostile enough to the Soviet Union on the one hand and not critical enough of the government's 'Fabian tastes' on the other. Foot felt that Orwell had no grasp of 'practical politics' (Foot 1987: 201). There is probably something in this view given that Foot's notion of 'practical politics' involved accepting a secret subvention of £3,000 from the viciously rightwing *Daily Express* no less to keep the newspaper afloat in 1951! If this had come out at the time both Foot and *Tribune* would have been finished, but it was successfully kept secret until the early 1970s (Taylor 1972: 598). Orwell also, it has to be said, objected to *Tribune's* strong support for the Zionist cause.

'THEY DON'T APPEAR TO BE FRIGHTENED'

To all intents and purposes, *Tribune's* pages were closed to Orwell's doubts concerning the performance of the Labour government so that he inevitably turned to *Partisan Review* to express his views. In the summer of 1946, the magazine published his initial assessment of the Labour government's performance. He recorded that the government's standing with the people was still 'good, and all the evidence in the form of local election and public opinion polls confirms this'. What he found both astonishing and disturbing, however, even given that change takes time, was 'how little change seems to have happened as yet in the structure of society'. There was, he supposed a 'drift towards Socialism, or at least towards state ownership' with the railways, for example, being taken out of private hands. The fact was, though, that the 'railway shareholders are being bought out at prices they would hardly get in the open market'. He went on:

> But in the social set-up there is no symptom by which one could infer that we are not living under a Conservative government. No move has been made against the House of Lords, for example, there has been no talk of disestablishing the Church, there has been little replacement of Tory ambassadors, service chiefs or other high officials, and if any effort is really being made to democratise education, it has borne no fruit as yet. Allowing for the general impoverishment, the upper classes are still living their accustomed life, and though they certainly dislike the Labour government, they don't appear to be frightened of it (*CWGO* 18: 286-287).

From this point of view, the upper class obviously had a much better appreciation of British Labourism and its limitations than Orwell did!

What perhaps pointed in the direction of his future trajectory was that even at this point, he identified 'the main danger to the government' as coming not from the 'upper class' but from the Communist Party, even though, as he acknowledged, it still only had 'a few score thousands' of members and supporters. While he did not think there was much opposition to 'Bevin's policies in

Greece and Indonesia', there was a danger that some 'calamity abroad – for instance, large-scale fighting in India' might play into the communists' hands (ibid). His exaggerated fear of domestic communism and of the international threat posed by the Soviet Union were, without any doubt, to contribute to pulling his politics to the right, but only in the sense that he became increasingly supportive of the Labour government even though it had disappointed his hopes for some sort of socialist revolution.

The best indication that he recognised how empty his illusions in Labourism had proven is provided once again in a contribution he made to *Partisan Review*. In 1947, he contributed to the magazine's 'The Future of Socialism' series along with Sidney Hook, Granville Hicks, Arthur Schlesinger Jr and Victor Serge. His contribution, 'Towards European Unity', that appeared in the July-August issue, makes absolutely clear that he did not see the Labour government as advancing the socialist cause (*CWGO* 19: 163-167). This has not been picked up on to the extent to which it should have been both because the article appeared in a US magazine and because he does not even mention the government. Nevertheless, if he had believed that the Labour government was carrying through a socialist revolution one would have expected him to use the article as an opportunity to celebrate its achievements and recommend its example. He does no such thing. Instead, he makes clear that he considered the position of socialists – and this is when Labour were in power with an overwhelming majority in the House of Commons – as being 'all but hopeless' with the 'chances against us' (ibid). He made absolutely clear that he was still a socialist and still believed that socialism was possible. As far as he was concerned though, 'socialism cannot properly be said to be established until it is worldwide', but a start had to be made somewhere and from this point of view, 'a socialist United States of Europe seems to me the only worth-while political objective today'. At this point in time, he still considered that Britain had to get free of the United States: the fact that it was 'almost a dependency' was an obstacle to any hope of Socialism. At no point in this article does he give any indication whatever that he considered the Labour government as in anyway advancing the socialist cause. And this article is without any doubt one of his last considered political statements (ibid).

Why then did Orwell continue to support the Attlee government? He certainly expressed private reservations, complaining on his death-bed, for example, that he had 'expected something more spectacular than Attlee's England of the Beveridge Plan and Welfare State' and had hoped for a 'manifest revolution' instead. Indeed, he complained that there were 'far too many visible signs of wealth in London ... all these Rolls-Royces' (Spender 1979: 75). Instead of breaking with the government, however, he had remained loyal because he had come to the conclusion that Britain was engaged in a struggle for survival and in these circumstances 'the struggle between collectivism and laissez faire is secondary'. Once again he put these arguments forward in a US magazine, *Commentary*, in many ways a Jewish sister magazine to *Partisan Review*. In October 1948, it published his 'Britain's Struggle for Survival: The Labor Government after Three Years' (*CWGO* 19: 436-443). This article provides an interesting instance of how support for Labourism pulls even a socialist like Orwell to the right. The contrast with his stance in 1941-1942 is quite stark. Then the struggle for survival required a socialist solution. But in 1948, with a Labour government in power, the struggle for socialism has to be put aside. Instead, the working class has got to knuckle down and work harder, cut levels of absenteeism, stop going on strike and accept 'austerity'. He even contemplates the need for forced labour although called 'by some more soothing name'. He actually argues that one reason why a Conservative government would be a disaster is that it would not be able to persuade the working class to make the necessary sacrifices and would plunge the country into class war (ibid).

And another way in which his support for Labourism pulled him to the right was his shameful involvement with the Labour government's Information Research Department (IRD). The IRD had been established to conduct a covert anti-communist propaganda offensive, although from a social democratic rather than a pro-capitalist position. Orwell's association with the organisation saw him not only allow his last two novels to be used to this end, but he also provided the IRD with a list of people he considered unreliable. This was, in itself, a serious mistake, but the list also showed that he had an unsavoury side.[3]

CONCLUSION

At the time of his death, Orwell's politics were being pulled in contradictory directions. He was still a socialist and was opposed to the imposition of any British McCarthyism. But he also supported the Labour government's 'austerity' programme and had made clear his support for the alliance with the United States against the Soviet Union up to and including war. Would he have responded to the Korean War by supporting or opposing British involvement? What would he have made of Bevan's resignation from the government? We have no way of knowing. What is clear, however, is that at the time of his death he still considered himself a socialist

NOTES

[1] *CWGO* refers throughout to Davison, Peter (ed.) (1998) *The Complete Works of George Orwell*, 20 Vols, London: Secker and Warburg

[2] See Newsinger, John (1999) *Orwell's Politics*, London: Macmillan

[3] See the discussion in Newsinger, John (2018 forthcoming) *'Hope Lies in the Proles': Orwell and the Left*, London: Pluto

REFERENCES

Bew, John (2016) *Citizen Clem*, London: Riverrun

Brockway, Fenner (1937) *The Truth about Barcelona*, London: Independent Labour Party

Brockway, Fenner (1938) *Workers' Front*, London: Secker and Warburg

Foot, Michael (1987) *Loyalists and Loners*, London: HarperCollins

Fyvel, Tosco (1971) The Years at *Tribune*, Miriam Gross (ed.) *The World of George Orwell*, London: Weidenfeld and Nicolson

Spender, Stephen (1979) *The Thirties and After: Poetry, Politics, People 1930s-1970s*, New York: Vintage

Taylor, A. J. P. (1972) *Beaverbrook*, London: Penguin

NOTE ON THE CONTRIBUTOR

John Newsinger is Professor of Modern History at Bath Spa University. His latest book, *Hope Lies in the Proles: Orwell and the Left*, is due out early in 2018.

ARTICLE

ARTICLE

Leaders and their Qualities:
Orwell on Cripps, Bevan and Attlee

PHILIP BOUNDS

Philip Bounds argues that Orwell's journalistic comments about some of the Labour leaders of his time 'emit a powerful sense of what he expected a radical tribune to be like'.

Recent developments on the left in Britain have focused many people's minds on the issue of political leadership. The election of Jeremy Corbyn as leader of the Labour Party in 2015 has engendered an especially urgent debate. Recognising that Corbyn and his allies are among the most radical leaders in Labour's history, journalists, academics and activists have begun to pose some crucial questions. In an age such as ours, which characteristics do Labour leaders need to possess if they are to compete successfully in the media marketplace? What combination of qualities will enable them not merely to win public support but to remain true to their radical instincts?

One writer to whom we can turn for help with questions such as these is George Orwell. Although his commentaries on political events focused more on policies than on individuals, they contained some penetrating remarks about a handful of the leading Labour politicians of the 1940s. There is nothing approaching a theory of leadership in his work, but his casual asides about Labour leaders emit a powerful sense of what he expected a radical tribune to be like. As with so many other aspects of his work, Orwell's journalistic remarks about politicians such as of Stafford Cripps, Aneurin Bevan and Clement Attlee provide an excellent starting point for a broader debate.

STAFFORD CRIPPS: THE ASCETIC OUTSIDER

The first leading Labour politician to whom Orwell paid serious attention was Stafford Cripps.[1] His interest in Cripps was largely an expression of his idiosyncratic response to the outbreak of the Second World War. As is well known, Orwell was convinced in the early stages of the war that Britain could not successfully resist fascism without simultaneously transforming the entire social order. In *The Lion and Unicorn* and in a series of shorter works (Orwell 1941), he argued that British capitalism had come to impede military efficiency and needed to be replaced by socialist planning.[2] It was in this context that Cripps seemed so significant. Having led the quasi-Marxist Socialist League in the 1930s, Cripps had been expelled from the Labour Party in 1939 for endorsing the Communist Party's call for a 'Popular Front' against fascism. This meant that he spent the early war years as a sort of unaffiliated radical-at-large, serving the government in various capacities but belonging to no political party.[3] His public reputation was so high that many people regarded him as the obvious choice to replace a beleaguered Churchill as Prime Minister. Orwell's belief was that Cripps had all the necessary qualities to oversee the sort of revolutionary war strategy he favoured, resisting fascism and overthrowing capitalism at one and the same time.[4]

At one level, Orwell's faith in Cripps grew out of his sense that no one was better placed to cement Britain's military alliances. As a long-term apologist for the USSR and an enthusiastic supporter of the Indian independence movement, Cripps could use his ideological kinship with men like Stalin and Gandhi to persuade them to support the war effort. (In the event, Cripps negotiated successfully with Stalin but much less successfully with Gandhi.) More importantly, Orwell also argued that Cripps's temporary status as an independent radical gave him a unique opportunity to stimulate fundamental change. The revolutionary potential of the wartime situation could only be realised if someone appealed to the British people over the heads of the existing party leaders. As a highly prestigious politician whose expulsion from the Labour Party had temporarily freed him from its ideological and organisational constraints, Cripps was extremely well-placed to mobilise ordinary people in support of socialist ends. At the core of his political appeal was his highly unusual public image, which (or so Orwell implied) effectively prefigured the sort of ideological, cultural and ethical changes which the socialist project required. With his reputation for high-minded asceticism and his famously self-denying lifestyle, Cripps powerfully dramatised the need for a clean break with capitalist materialism. Indeed, there are places in Orwell's wartime writings when he comes close to portraying Cripps as a sort of English Gandhi, steering the people towards new and more ethical forms of living through the exemplary force of his own personal example:

ARTICLE

> Sir Stafford Cripps has long been recognised as the ablest man in the British Socialist movement, and he is respected for his absolute integrity even by those who are at the opposite pole from him politically. ... In spite of this [i.e. his prestigious legal career and his experience in government], he has always lived with extreme simplicity and has given away most of his earnings at the Bar to the cause of Socialism and to the support of his weekly Socialist paper, 'The Tribune'. He is a man of great personal austerity,

a vegetarian, a teetotaller and a devout practising Christian. So simple are his manners that he is to be seen every morning having his breakfast in a cheap London eating house, among working men and office employees (Orwell 1942a: 224-225).

Although Orwell's admiration for Cripps was undoubtedly sincere, there is some evidence that his attitude towards him was more ambivalent than it sometimes seemed. The passage just quoted was part of a BBC broadcast to India in March 1942. Written in the week that the British government dispatched Cripps to Bombay to negotiate with Gandhi and other nationalist leaders, its purpose was to convince sceptical Indian listeners that Cripps was a man to be trusted. This accounts for its rather uncharacteristic note of reverence and its implicit comparison between Cripps and Gandhi. Elsewhere in his writings of the time, Orwell spoke of Cripps in a much cooler register. For example, in one of his regular 'London Letters' to the left-wing New York magazine, *Partisan Review*, he praised Cripps for remaining true to his political principles. But he also observed: 'I can't yet say with certainty that Cripps is not merely a second-rate figure to whom the public have tied their hopes, a sort of bubble blown by popular discontent' (Orwell 1942d: 305). The disjuncture between the two pieces – one slightly artificial in its respectfulness, the other bordering on cynicism – hints at the intense psychological pressures which eventually led Orwell to leave the BBC and resume his membership of the 'agin the government' awkward squad.[5]

ANEURIN BEVAN: THE WORKING CLASS *TRIBUNE*

The war did not unfold as Orwell had anticipated. It was clear by the middle of 1942 that the British people did not need to abolish capitalism in order to defeat Nazism. Instead of being swept to the premiership at the head of an insurgent popular movement, Cripps joined Churchill's coalition government and eschewed the role of left-wing firebrand. Orwell did not take a serious interest in another Labour leader until his friend Aneurin Bevan became Minister of Health in the first Attlee administration.[6] Commissioned by the *Observer* to write an anonymous profile of Bevan in October 1945, Orwell expressed the cautious hope that his subject would succeed where others had failed and oversee a transformation of working class living standards (Orwell 1945).

A superficial reading of the piece might see it as a slightly naive celebration of Bevan's proletarian roots. Evoking his impoverished upbringing in South Wales and paying tribute to his early work as a trade union official and local councillor, Orwell commended Bevan not merely for thinking like a working man but also for feeling like one. By virtue of his unlettered background, or so it was implied, Bevan was insulated against the temptation to compromise by a powerfully intuitive understanding of working class needs. In reality, however, Orwell admired Bevan not only for his working class virtues but for the way he combined them with some altogether rarer qualities. The first of these was a sort of fruitful turbulence of mind. Pilloried by Churchill at the height of the war as an 'architect of disloyalty' (quoted in Orwell 1945: 310), Bevan was widely regarded as a mercurial, emotionally unpredictable figure with a combustible temper. While conceding that his emotional unsteadiness had sometimes been the cause of 'irresponsibility' and extremism, Orwell also seemed to see it as a precondition of his political creativity. It was almost as if Bevan, exasperated beyond endurance by the cross-party verities of the age, used his fits of temper as a means of sloughing off orthodoxy and breaking through to new and more progressive habits of thought. Closely linked to this desire to see things anew were his 'respect for the intellect' and his concern with the integrity of the English language. In a passage which probably drew on his memories of working with Bevan on *Tribune*, Orwell noted that:

> Those who have worked with him in a journalistic capacity have remarked with pleasure and astonishment that here at last is a politician who knows that literature exists and will even hold up work for five minutes to discuss a point of style (ibid: 312).

Compliments like these did not simply reflect the desire of a literary man to pay tribute to an unusually literate politician. They also hinted at Orwell's sense that leaders like Bevan had a crucial role to play in resisting the cultural-linguistic malaise of the totalitarian age. From the mid-1930s onwards, Orwell increasingly came to feel that the onset of political barbarism in Europe had corrupted everyday language (see, *inter alia*, Orwell 1944, 1946). Anxious to distract people's attention from the horror of their actions, authoritarian leaders and their hired propagandists had eschewed plain language in favour of impenetrable euphemisms: The mass murder of civilians was now described as 'pacification', the extra-judicial suppression of political opponents as 'elimination of unreliable elements' (Orwell 1946: 428). Quite apart from obscuring people's understanding of what was going on, the new political language robbed them of their intellectual vitality. No one, or so Orwell argued, could be expected to think clearly when the only words at his disposal were intended to conceal meaning rather than reveal it. When he drew attention to Bevan's extraordinary facility for expressing political truths clearly and persuasively, Orwell was perhaps implying that the linguistic crisis had to be confronted not merely by beleaguered intellectuals like himself but by the few remaining politicians who retained a capacity for plain-speaking. Here, again, Bevan's working class background probably seemed significant. Like a number of other socialist intellectuals of his time (see, *inter alia*, Fox 1948 [1937]), Orwell thought that working people were more likely than their social superiors to use language in a vividly concrete manner (Orwell 1947: 34n). As such, he might well have believed that Bevan – deeply rooted in the culture of the Welsh coalfields – could draw strength in his battle against obscurity from South Wales's immense reserves of proletarian lucidity.

The most surprising passage in Orwell's article described Bevan's way of relating to other people. In spite of portraying Bevan as an uncompromising socialist with a pronounced tendency to extremism, Orwell made a point of insisting that he lacked 'any feeling of personal grievance against society' (Orwell 1945: 311). Naturally and authentically egalitarian in his attitudes, he felt at ease with people from all backgrounds and treated everyone in the same way. He was entirely free – or so Orwell implied – of the hack socialist's regrettable tendency to nurture a ferocious hatred of the rich and a sentimental reverence for the masses. Virtually everyone who knew him referred to him simply as 'Nye'. Although Orwell did not dwell on the political consequences of Bevan's egalitarian geniality, he probably saw it as a valuable specific against the Stalinist left's toxic blend of self-righteousness and authoritarianism. Grimly aware of the way that class hatred had fuelled political repression in the USSR and elsewhere, Orwell was effectively saying that a socialist politician should combine a clear-sighted awareness of his opponents' methods and motives with a scrupulous respect for their humanity. Bevan's great virtue was that he had the instincts of a class warrior and the conscience of a nineteenth-century liberal.

CLEMENT ATTLEE: THE UNFLAPPABLE PRIME MINISTER

Orwell's respect for Cripps and Bevan grew out of his belief that they were exceptional men who prefigured the socialist future in their everyday attitudes and habits of behaviour. By contrast, his admiration for Clement Attlee – the other leading Labour politician whom he commented on in detail – reflected the widely-held perception that Attlee's most noteworthy characteristic was his sheer *ordinariness*.[7] In a 1948 review of Roy Jenkins's 'interim biography' of the then-Prime Minister, Orwell portrayed Attlee as the archetype of a certain sort of stolid, pedestrian but utterly reliable middle class Englishman. Educated at a minor public school and exceptional neither in intellect nor in sporting prowess, Attlee had thrived in the Labour Party because his 'unspectacular qualities' had enabled him to 'keep his feet through very difficult times and to out-stay many more brilliant men' (Orwell 1948: 398). The implied argument here was that the socialist project required solidly dependable leaders as much as brilliantly inspiring ones. When a radical government was seeking to transfer power from one class to another, the role of men like Attlee – sensible, unflappable, conservative with a small 'c' – was to calm the public's nerves and to reassure them that the immemorial rhythms of everyday life went on as before. On a related note, Orwell also implied that Attlee's strengths as a left-wing politician derived from the fact that his socialism had been learned through experience rather than drummed into him by his background. Noting that Attlee had been a staunch Tory as a young man, he reminded his readers that the future Labour leader had only gone over to the left while working in a public school mission in impoverished Limehouse, east London. The strength of his commitment to the cause – his unshakeable belief in the necessity of socialism – arose from the traumatising clash between his inherited ideology and the conditions he encountered when first set down in a working class environment. Shaken by the failure of Toryism to explain or offer solutions to poverty and mass unemployment, Attlee embraced socialist ideas because they helped to reconnect him to a world he no longer understood. Indeed, in an aside which anticipated the themes of today's Blue Labour thinkers (see Geary and Pabst 2015), Orwell argued that it was Attlee's almost parochial concern for the people of Limehouse that made him such an effective radical tribune. Unlike some of his more cosmopolitan colleagues in the Labour Party, Attlee had served the same community for more than forty years and, in so doing, had convinced ordinary people that socialists could be trusted to fight their corner. His instinctive suspicion of the far left, exemplified by his dislike of the Communist Party's Popular Front policy in the 1930s, only reinforced his reputation for reliability and common sense.[8]

CONCLUSION

It would be wrong to attach too much significance to Orwell's scattered remarks about Cripps, Bevan and Attlee. His writings on the leading Labour politicians of the day were largely a product of journalistic necessity. They were not part of a sustained effort to understand the role of leaders in progressive movements or to identify a radical tribune's ideal characteristics. Nevertheless, his largely *ad hoc* comments give us a powerful sense of the sort of qualities he expected Labour leaders to possess. Abstracting from his particular remarks – and seeking to infer general principles from some highly compressed formulations – it is possible to argue that Orwell held the following views:

(1) If fundamental social change is to be achieved, there is a need for leaders who are unconstrained by long-term membership of the Labour Party hierarchy. Labour's established leaders are too beholden to parliamentary traditions. Outsiders are better able to sink deep roots in working class communities and encourage them to fight for socialism.

(2) Labour needs more leaders who are either from working class backgrounds or have substantial experience of working class conditions. The great virtue of working class leaders like Bevan is that their understanding of the case for socialism is emotional as well as intellectual.

(3) Labour's leaders need to anticipate the ethical and cultural norms of socialist society in their everyday behaviour. Crippsian asceticism and Bevanite egalitarianism are a powerful means of weaning people off capitalist ideology and pointing them towards the socialist future.

(4) Radical leaders have linguistic responsibilities as well as more directly political ones. They must challenge the linguistic corruption of the age and use words clearly, accessibly and honestly.

(5) The culture of the left has been disfigured by class hatred and intolerance of political opponents. In a spirit of genuine egalitarianism, Labour leaders should avoid dehumanising their opponents and take care to respect their rights.

(6) The attempt to build a socialist society necessarily breeds widespread anxiety. There is a role for leaders whose level-headed ordinariness and respect for tradition serve to reassure the public that change is not occurring too chaotically.

How relevant are Orwell's ideas to the current debate about the nature of the Labour leadership? His sense of what a people's tribune should look like is certainly an attractive one. After decades in which Labour leaders have specialised in selling their supporters short, Orwell's vision of a collective of liberal-minded outsiders challenging the *status quo*, waging war on linguistic corruption and prefiguring the socialist future resonates with many of us. The problem with his account of the Labour leadership is not so much one of substance as of context. Writing primarily about individuals, Orwell sometimes gives the impression that the qualities of political leaders are either innate or shaped by their unique personal histories. The obvious objection to this is that it ignores the way that leaders are affected by particular organisational forms and political cultures.

Most obviously, Orwell never addresses the role of the Labour Party's constitution in promoting certain styles of leadership and retarding others. Nowhere in his work is there a proto-Bennite discussion of how leaders should be nominated, who should vote for them (and how their votes should be weighted), how policy should be formulated and how leaders can be held accountable by their supporters. On the other hand, it is easy to see how his broader writings on the political culture of the left can be used to fill out his conception of radical leadership. Especially relevant here are his efforts in the early 1940s to reconcile democratic socialism with patriotism. In seeking to ensure that liberal-minded people such as Bevan and Attlee took precedence over the labour movement's more authoritarian figures, Orwell argued that socialism must ultimately be seen as a twentieth century adaptation of a unique, long-established and essentially libertarian English identity. If socialists and their leaders are to be insulated against the temptations of Stalinism, it is necessary – or so Orwell believed – to build a political culture which portrays the modern left as the proud inheritor of a longstanding English preoccupation with individual liberty. At a time when the British people's decision to liberate themselves from the European Union yields new opportunities to reforge the culture of the left, Orwell's appeal to radical patriotism is as relevant as it has ever been. Whether Jeremy Corbyn and his allies can take advantage of the new situation is another matter entirely.

NOTES

[1] Stafford Cripps (1889-1952). Labour MP for Bristol South East, 1931-1950. Best known for his period as Chancellor of the Exchequer, 1947-1950

[2] For Orwell's revolutionary war strategy, see, *inter alia*, Newsinger 2001: 61n; Bounds 2009: 39n

[3] Cripps served as the British ambassador to the USSR between 1940 and 1942. After returning to Britain, he joined the Churchill coalition and served successively as Lord Privy Seal, Leader of the House of Commons and Minister for Aircraft Production. In 1942, he travelled to India to try to persuade its nationalist leaders to support the war effort

[4] References to Cripps are scattered throughout Orwell's writings of the early war years. The most important references to him can be found in Orwell 1942a, 1942b, 1943c, 1942d, 1942e

[5] By the middle of 1942, Orwell had two reasons for supposing that Cripps had probably blown his opportunity to lead an anti-capitalist revolt in Britain. The first was that Cripps's credibility had been undermined by his decision to join the government; the second was that his reputation for getting results had foundered on the failure of his talks with Gandhi, Nehru and other nationalist leaders in India. Insofar as Orwell still paid any attention to Cripps after that point, it is clear that his attitude towards him remained profoundly ambivalent. This comes across with particular vividness in the diary entries which describe his two meetings with Cripps in May and June 1942. On the one hand, Orwell expressed his concern that Cripps had now become an example of 'the official mind, which sees everything as a problem in administration' and fails to take account of basic human motivations (Orwell 1942e: 485-486). On the other hand, Orwell claimed to be 'rather well impressed' with Cripps's personal qualities, describing him as 'more approachable and easy-going than I had expected' and 'very human and willing to listen' (Orwell 1942e: 481/485). In the final analysis, Orwell came to admire Cripps the man more than he admired Cripps the politician

[6] Aneurin Bevan (1897-1960). Labour MP for Ebbw Vale, 1929-1960. Oversaw the creation of the National Health Service in his capacity as Minister of Health, 1945-1951. For some brief but illuminating remarks about Orwell's relationship with Bevan, see Foot 1999: 167-168; Campbell 1987: 106-107; Thomas-Symonds 2016: 97-98

[7] Clement Attlee (1883-1967). Labour MP for Limehouse (1922-1950) and Walthamstow West (1950-1955). Prime Minister of the United Kingdom, 1945-1951

[8] Orwell had not always felt the cautious admiration for Attlee which came across in his review of Jenkins's biography. In a scathing entry in his war-time diary in May 1942, he went so far as to say that Attlee reminded him of 'a recently dead fish, before it has had time to stiffen' (Orwell 1942e: 481). Like so many other people, he only came to appreciate Attlee's political gifts after seeing him serve as Prime Minister

ARTICLE

PHILIP BOUNDS

REFERENCES

Bounds, Philip (2009) *Orwell and Marxism: The Political and Cultural Thinking of George Orwell*, London: I. B. Tauris

Campbell, John (1987) *Nye Bevan and the Mirage of British Socialism*, London: Weidenfeld and Nicolson

Foot, Michael (1999) *Aneurin Bevan 1897-1960*, Brivati, Brian (ed.) London: Indigo

Fox, Ralph (1948 [1937]) *The Novel and the People*, London: The Cobbett Press

Geary, Ian and Pabst, Adrian (2015) *Blue Labour: Forging a New Politics*, London: I. B. Tauris

Newsinger, John (2001) *Orwell's Politics*, Basingstoke: Palgrave

Orwell, George (1941) *The Lion and the Unicorn: Socialism and the English Genius*, Davison, Peter (ed.) (2000) *Collected Works of George Orwell* (hereafter *CWGO*) Vol. 12, London: Secker and Warburg pp 391-434

Orwell, George (1942a) Weekly news review, 14, 14 March, Davison, Peter (ed.) (2001) *CWGO*, Vol. 13, London: Secker and Warburg pp 224-227

Orwell, George (1942b) Marathi newsletter, 3, 19 March, Davison, Peter (ed.) (2001) *CWGO*, Vol. 13, London: Secker and Warburg pp 234-235

Orwell, George (1942c) Weekly news review, 15, 21 March, Davison, Peter (ed.) (2001) *CWGO*, Vol. 13, London: Secker and Warburg pp 236-239

Orwell, George (1942d) London letter 8 May 1942, *Partisan Review*, July-August, Davison, Peter (ed.) (2001) *CWGO*, Vol. 13, London: Secker and Warburg pp 302-309

Orwell, George (1942e) War-time diary, 14 March-15 November, Orwell, Sonia and Angus, Ian (eds) (1970) *The Collected Essays, Journalism and Letters of George Orwell, Volume 2: My Country Right or Left 1940-1943*, Harmondsworth: Penguin pp 464-508

Orwell, George (1944) Propaganda and demotic speech, *Persuasion*, Summer, Vol. 2, No. 2, Davison, Peter (ed.) (2001) *CWGO*, Vol. 16, London: Secker and Warburg pp 310-316

Orwell, George (1945) Aneurin Bevan, profile, *Observer*, 14 October, Davison, Peter (ed.) (2001) *CWGO*, Vol. 17, London: Secker and Warburg pp 310-313

Orwell, George (1946) Politics and the English language, *Horizon*, April, Davison, Peter (ed.) (2001) *CWGO*, Vol. 17, London: Secker and Warburg pp 421-432

Orwell, George (1947) *The English People*, London: Collins

Orwell, George (1948) Review of *Mr. Attlee: An Interim Biography*, by Roy Jenkins, *Observer*, 4 July, Davison, Peter (ed.) (2001) *CWGO*, Vol. 19, London: Secker and Warburg pp 398-399

Thomas-Symonds, Nicklaus (2016) *Nye: The Political Life of Aneurin Bevan*, London: I. B. Tauris

NOTE ON THE CONTRIBUTOR

Philip Bounds is a historian, journalist and critic. He holds a PhD in Politics from the University of Wales and has published widely on the history of the British left. His books include *Orwell and Marxism* (2009), *British Communism and the Politics of Literature* (2012) and *Notes from the End of History* (2014).

PAPER

So What Sort of Democratic Socialist Was He?

PAUL ANDERSON

George Orwell's relationship to the British Labour Party was ambiguous. There is no doubt that he was a democratic socialist or that he supported Labour in the 1940s – but he developed his ideas over time, and in the 1930s was a revolutionary socialist opponent of Labour. He changed his mind because of the outbreak of the Second World War, when he backed the Allied cause (with Labour), and his new orientation was reinforced by the British government's failure to deal with Indian demands for independence. That led to his joining the Labour weekly Tribune, *and he remained a* Tribune *socialist until his death in 1950. It is a mistake to see* Animal Farm *and* Nineteen Eighty-Four *as signs that Orwell had abandoned his socialist commitment.*

Keywords: George Orwell, Labour, socialism, communism, anarchism, *Tribune, Partisan Review*

No political writer of the 20th century has been subject to more analysis, controversy and speculation than George Orwell – and for good reason. Many see Orwell as the greatest political writer in the English language of the past 200 years, a consummate stylist, always direct and provocative, and many of his big concerns have continuing resonance even though he died nearly 70 years ago. He wrote a lot, and in a multitude of genres: fiction, criticism, reportage, poetry, polemical essays and columns. His conception of what is political was breathtakingly broad, he changed his mind over time (and in public), and there are innumerable tensions and contradictions in his life and work.

Since his death in 1950, partisans of every political tendency, apart from fascists and Stalinist communists, have tried to claim Orwell as one of their own. Orwell stated in 1946:

> Every line of serious work that I have written since 1936 has been written, directly or indirectly, against totalitarianism and for democratic socialism, as I understand it (1998 [1946a]).

PAUL ANDERSON

But that has not stopped anyone trying to enter the Orwell appropriation industry. Some (most recently Peter Wilkin) have made a great deal of Orwell's reported self-description in the early 1930s as a 'Tory anarchist' (Wilkin 2013). Others, following Leopold Labedz in a feature in *Encounter* more than 30 years ago (Labedz 1984), have detected signs in his late-1940s writings, in particular *Nineteen Eighty-Four*, that he was losing faith in democratic socialism and have speculated that he would have become a staunch Cold War liberal (or perhaps even some sort of conservative) had he lived through the 1950s. Still others seem to believe that no one who enjoyed the small pleasures of English everyday life as Orwell did – afternoon tea, warm beer, the crime and sex scandals reported in the Sunday popular press – could really be only the most milk-and-water kind of socialist (Colls 2013).

Some of this is legitimate. There are ambiguities in Orwell's published work and more in his private correspondence and behaviour. There are indications in his letters that by 1948-1949 he had grown weary of the British left (though also plenty of signs that he still considered himself part of it) – and, of course, there is the infamous list he gave to Celia Kirwan, a friend then working for a newly created government propaganda operation, of communist-sympathetic writers and artists he thought it should not hire (Anderson 2014: 93). But there are limits to what we can extrapolate. We shall never know what Orwell would have said after he died, and it is asinine to claim that Orwell was never a serious socialist because he was friends with anarchists and Tories, wrote a not completely dismissive review of Friedrich von Hayek or took James Burnham seriously. There is no evidence at all that he ever gave up on socialism. And the names he gave Kirwan constitute less a McCarthyite blacklist than a written-down version of what every commissioning editor on a political publication keeps in the back of his or her head. Which is not to say that he should have handed it over, just that it does not invalidate Orwell's claim to have been a democratic socialist for most of his short adult life.

So let's take him for a democratic socialist. But what sort of democratic socialist was he?

ORWELL'S SOCIALISM IN THE THIRTIES
On this question, we should be grateful to several people for clearing detritus over the years, but none more so than John Newsinger, whose *Orwell's Politics* (1999) makes it crystal clear how Eric Blair of St Cyprian's prep school, Eton College and the Indian imperial police became a radical socialist journalist and novelist in the early 1930s – in part through his direct experience of British colonialism and his participant-observation of the lives of the poor in Britain and France, but also through his involvement with the intellectuals around the Independent Labour Party review, the *Adelphi*, edited by the radical pacifist poet and critic John Middleton Murry.

Newsinger's account of Orwell's political journey through the 1930s and early 1940s is difficult to fault. He situates Orwell as a player – at first marginal, later central – in a long-lost left intellectual and political culture. The ILP was hostile both to the dirty compromises of the Labour Party's electoral and trade union politics and to the much dirtier games of the Moscow-affiliated Communist Party of Great Britain as it danced to Stalin's tune (though it was not averse to joining forces with Labour and the CP to oppose 'fascism and war'). The ILP had disaffiliated from Labour in 1932, and Orwell did not join it until 1938, after the ILP had more-or-less given up on the idea that it could form an anti-fascist united front with the CP because of the CP's support for Stalin's show trials and its perfidy over Spain (where those under Moscow's command effectively destroyed the revolutionary left on the Republican side). But it was through Orwell's ILP contacts that in 1935 he met the northern English industrial workers he wrote about in *The Road to Wigan Pier* and in 1936 joined the far-left (and Trotskyist-influenced) POUM militia in Spain, which gave us *Homage to Catalonia*.

The ILP after disaffiliation from Labour was a strange beast. It was a shadow of its former self, reduced in membership to the low thousands and represented in parliament by just five MPs, led by James Maxton. It had lost many of its most important intellectuals and no longer had the must-read left weekly of the day as it had in the 1920s when Clifford Allen and H. N. Brailsford edited its *New Leader*. (The 1930s was the decade of the *New Statesman*, edited by the Soviet fellow-traveller Kingsley Martin.) But the ILP had a cachet, nevertheless, as the keeper of the socialist flame, and after disaffiliating from Labour in 1932 appeared refreshed and principled: a revolutionary party, no less. The *Adelphi* crew was hardly the Bolshevik leadership of 1917 – it was more sandal-wearing days of discussion in medium-sized country houses near Letchworth and Colchester owned by rich sympathisers – but it was open and fertile. Orwell made the ILP his political home for the best part of a decade.

The Orwell of the 1930s was as sceptical about the Labour Party as any ILPer – which is hardly surprising. There was little about Labour in the 1930s to attract anyone without a career as a trade union bureaucrat or local government representative (or both). Following two spells of at-best-lacklustre minority government, the first in 1924, the second from 1929, Labour had been utterly humiliated in the 1931 general election.

The debacle came about after its leader and Prime Minister, Ramsay MacDonald, abandoned the party in the face of a largely media-created budget crisis. MacDonald and his chancellor of the exchequer, Philip Snowden, formed a National government in coalition with the Tories rather than refuse to impose massive cuts

PAUL ANDERSON

to balance the books. Led by Arthur Henderson after MacDonald jumped ship, Labour won just 52 seats out of 625 in the Commons, down 225 on its 1929 result, with the Tories taking 470, up 210. Henderson was among the Labour candidates who lost in the Tory landslide which, nevertheless, kept MacDonald as Prime Minister, the leader of a 13-strong National Labour contingent.

In the wake of the defeat, Labour all but imploded. A majority of the ILP voted to disaffiliate from Labour (of which it had formed the activist base in much of the country, with MacDonald and Snowden its key leaders only a decade before). The parliamentary Labour Party was reduced to electing George Lansbury, the veteran pacifist left-wing MP for Bow and Bromley in the East End of London, already in his 70s, much-loved but completely ineffectual, as leader.

It was not until 1934 that there was any sign of Labour electoral recovery – when Labour won a majority on the London County Council for the first time, under Herbert Morrison – and it took an extraordinary political coup (engineered by the leader of the Transport and General Workers' Union, Ernest Bevin) to get rid of Lansbury before the 1935 general election. Labour did better than in 1931, under Clement Attlee, but increased its representation in the Commons only to 154.

On the ground, Labour was for the most part sclerotic throughout the 1930s – the party of local trade union bigwigs on the trades council that mobilised only at election time, complacent and parochial, culturally conservative. The activist left among individual party members in the constituencies, largely comprising ex-ILPers organised in the Socialist League (led from 1933 by the immensely rich barrister and MP for Bristol East, Stafford Cripps, and Labour-affiliated until 1937), was marginal and fractious (Pimlott 1977).

Orwell's take on 1930s Labour pervades everything he wrote on Britain in the period, but it is summed up in his remarks in *The Road to Wigan Pier*, researched in 1936 and published in 1937, on 'the type who becomes a Labour MP or a high-up trade union official':

> This last type is one of the most desolating spectacles the world contains. He has been picked out to fight for his mates, and all it means to him is a soft job and the chance of bettering himself (Orwell 1998 [1937]).

The Road to Wigan Pier was excoriated by left critics when published for its supposedly snobbish antipathy to the working class – and Orwell's publisher, Victor Gollancz, disagreed with it enough to add an introduction disassociating himself from Orwell's arguments in the second part of the book. It is usually seen by commentators as a vicious attack on sandal-wearing vegetarian leftists, but is just as critical (if not more so) of the complacency of official Labour. The book became a best-seller and continues to work as a plea for the left to get real about the conditions of the people it purports to represent. It demands rejection of illusions – not just the self-deception of a radical left that, starry-eyed about the prospect of revolution, knows nothing of working class everyday life, but also the Labour narrative of everything going swimmingly in this great movement of ours. It is no surprise, as the CP used to say in the 1930s, that Orwell refers to Morrison's LCC only to note its meanness towards tramps, or that there is no evidence that he even voted in the 1935 general election, when Labour lost the inner-London constituency in Camden where he lived.

Orwell during the 1930s was never at ease with what Marxist writers have long dismissed as 'Labourism' – the party's hodge-podge of pragmatic incremental social-democratic reformism and trade union leaders' self-interest. Like others in and around the post-disaffiliation ILP, he saw himself as a revolutionary socialist (even if he had little but scorn for a lot of professed revolutionaries even in the ILP). And if Labour was where the workers were to be found – mostly – and was generally preferable to the Tories when it came to voting, Labour's failure to articulate a properly socialist programme, the conservatism of its trade union base and its plodding electoralism were anathema.

But the main problem with Labour for Orwell was that it was preparing for war. As he put it in 1938:

> The ILP is the only British party – at any rate the only one large enough to be worth considering – which aims at anything I should regard as socialism. I do not mean that I have lost all faith in the Labour Party. My most earnest hope is that the Labour Party will win a clear majority in the next general election. But we know what the history of the Labour Party has been, and we know the terrible temptation of the present moment – the temptation to fling every principle overboard in order to prepare for an imperialist war. It is vitally necessary that there should be in existence some body of people who can be depended on, even in the face of persecution, not to compromise their socialist principles (Orwell 1998 [1938]).

AFTER THE ILP

Orwell's anti-war stance was always anti-imperialist rather than pacifist – unlike much of the ILP, which was straightforwardly pacifist. And Orwell abandoned his opposition to war, along with his affiliation to the ILP, after the announcement of the Hitler-Stalin pact of August 1939. In the wake of Hitler's invasion of Czechoslovakia, Moscow and Berlin agreed, apparently out of the blue, to non-belligerence and co-operation (and to carve up

PAUL ANDERSON

Poland and the rest of east-central Europe, though that was not obvious for a few more weeks). It was a shamelessly cynical deal that made war all-but-inevitable between Nazi Germany and the major western European democratic powers, Britain and France.

Orwell prepared to support the lesser evil. His account of his change of mind – an instant conversion after a premonitory dream on the night the pact was signed – should be taken with a large pinch of salt, but the shift was undoubtedly sudden and unexpected by his ILP and anarchist comrades. From the outbreak of war, Orwell supported the British war effort against Hitler and abjured the defeatists and pacifists of the left, remaining on good personal terms with most of his onetime political allies but directing polemical venom at the communists and others who had supped with the devil. From early 1940 he took up a position of 'revolutionary patriotism', backing the creation of the Home Guard as a would-be workers' militia that might just form the force to undertake a socialist revolution (Orwell 1998 [1940]).

For anyone alive today, the idea that 'Dad's Army' was a potentially revolutionary workers' militia seems faintly ridiculous – but Britain in 1940 was in a state of extraordinary political flux, and Orwell was not alone in his belief that radical socialist change was imminent (his view was shared, *inter alia*, by Francis Williams, former editor of the *Daily Herald* and a Labour loyalist who was later Clement Attlee's press secretary, and Tom Wintringham, a former International Brigades commander in Spain who had fallen out irrevocably with the CP). The failure of Britain's military involvement in western Europe had destroyed the credibility of the National government even before the fall of France in May 1940 – it was the disastrous Norway campaign that led to the collapse of the Chamberlain administration and Churchill's elevation to office with Labour backing – and through the Battle of Britain and the Blitz in 1940-1941 popular confidence in the political class, the 'Guilty Men' of Michael Foot, Frank Owen and Peter Howard's best-selling July 1940 polemical pamphlet, was at its lowest point ('Cato' 1940).

Orwell's sense that Britain was ripe for revolution faded as the war ground on – and so did his antipathy to Labour (though much more slowly). His revolutionary patriotism and disdain for Labour are still very much alive in *The Lion and the Unicorn*, written in autumn 1940 and published in February 1941 under the aegis of Searchlight Books, an initiative of the publisher Fredric Warburg (who had published *Homage to Catalonia*) and the young ex-ILP journalist, Tosco Fyvel:

> In England there is only one socialist party that has ever seriously mattered, the Labour Party. It has never been able to achieve any major change, because except in purely domestic matters it has

never possessed a genuinely independent policy. It was and is primarily a party of the trade unions, devoted to raising wages and improving working conditions. This meant that all through the critical years it was directly interested in the prosperity of British capitalism (Orwell 1998 [1941a]).

Later in the pamphlet he declares:

> Within a year, perhaps even within six months, we shall see the rise of something that has never existed before, a specifically *English* socialist movement. Hitherto there has been only the Labour Party, which was the creation of the working class but did not aim at any fundamental change, and Marxism, which was a German theory interpreted by Russians and unsuccessfully transplanted to England (ibid).

But by the time of 'Patriots and Revolutionaries' – one of two Orwell contributions to Victor Gollancz's Left Book Club edited collection of polemics against the Communist Party's 1939-41 defeatism, *Betrayal of the Left*, written only a couple of months after *The Lion and the Unicorn* (of which it is largely a rehash) and published a few weeks later, Orwell was of the view that the revolutionary moment of 1940 had passed (Orwell 1998 [1941b]). He saw signs of hope over the next two or three years of something of the same, notably in the summer of 1942, when he declared to the readers of *Partisan Review* in the US that 'people are now as fed up and as ready for a radical policy as they were at the time of Dunkirk, with the difference that they now have, or are inclined to think they have, a potential leader in Stafford Cripps. ... We are back to the "revolutionary situation" which existed but was not utilised' (Orwell 1998 [1942a]). But Orwell never returned to the insurgent optimism of 1940.

Orwell's enthusiasm for Cripps in *Partisan Review*, published by a group of Trotskyist-influenced (though increasingly post-Trotskyist) intellectuals in New York, was very guarded ('I can't yet say that Cripps is not a second-rate figure to whom the public have tied their hopes') and he qualified even that with contempt for Labour in 1940 ('no guts') and for Attlee (a 'tame cat'). But it was significant in Orwell's softening towards Labour.

Cripps had been expelled by Labour in 1939 for advocating an anti-fascist electoral popular front alliance between Labour, the Communist Party and Liberals, and had not been readmitted (unlike the MPs Aneurin Bevan and George Strauss, his most loyal lieutenants, who had supported him on the popular front). In 1940, Cripps had been sent to Moscow by Churchill as the British emissary most likely to convince Stalin that Britain was not unfriendly, and he had returned home in early 1942 – at the nadir of Britain's war

PAUL ANDERSON

effort, with the empire in the far-east cut apart by Japan and the Germans positioned to take Egypt – acclaimed as the man who 'got Russia on our side' (as Orwell described the popular perception). But Cripps remained a Labour figure despite being outside the party, as Orwell recognised. And for a short while, Cripps seemed the people's choice to take over from the flailing Churchill as wartime leader. Churchill cannily responded by making him a member of the war cabinet and then almost immediately packed him off to India to solve the most difficult problem confronting his government, converting Indian nationalists to the Allied cause against Japan with promises of jam tomorrow – a doomed effort that led directly to a resurgence of Indian nationalist demands for Britain to get out at once: the 'Quit India' movement of civil disobedience initiated in August 1942 by Mahatma Gandhi, which was met in turn by a vicious British programme of mass detentions.

Orwell was a long-standing opponent of British imperialism. Working at the BBC for its Far Eastern Service between 1941 and 1943, had little choice but to back the 'Cripps mission'. 'Everyone in Britain is delighted to see such an important mission as the one which Cripps in undertaking conferred upon a man whom even his critics admit to be gifted, trustworthy and self-sacrificing,' he said in his BBC weekly talk in March 1942 (Orwell 1998 [1942b]). But this was not just propaganda. Orwell believed Cripps was a man of goodwill who had been set up to fail by Churchill and Halifax, was sympathetic when he met him at a long private meeting in June 1942 ('About 2½ hours of it, with nothing to drink,' according to Orwell's diary, though Cripps was 'very human and willing to listen' (Orwell 1998 [1942c]) and saw Cripps's failure in India and the subsequent draconian response to Quit India as little short of disastrous. 'The way the British government is now behaving in India upsets me more than a military defeat,' he noted in his diary (Orwell 1998 [1942d]).

Orwell resolved to get out from the propaganda game, leave the BBC and finish his new novel, what became *Animal Farm*. And it was a Cripps initiative – though one of many years before, the weekly paper *Tribune* – that gave him his means of escape.

ORWELL AT *TRIBUNE*

Tribune had been set up by Cripps in 1937 as the organ of the Unity Campaign, the Socialist League's quixotic attempt to secure a united front of Labour, the ILP and the Communist Party 'against fascism and war'. The Unity Campaign was a fiasco – the Labour leadership rejected it and threw out the Socialist League in 1937, and the ILP and CP fell out over Spain and the Moscow trials – but *Tribune* survived precariously over the next couple of years, despite losing Cripps a small fortune, by becoming an adjunct of the Left Book Club and adopting an uncritically pro-Soviet popular-frontist line, with a secret member of the CP as editor, H. J. Hartshorn. Cripps had effectively withdrawn from the paper by late 1939, when he embarked on a bizarre, semi-official (but self-funded) world tour meeting key political leaders – taking in China, the Soviet Union and the United States – and he ceased any formal relationship with it in spring 1940 on being sent to Moscow by Churchill. His role as sugar daddy was taken over by George Strauss, Labour MP for North Lambeth since 1935, who owed his considerable wealth to his family's metal merchant business, while Aneurin Bevan, Labour MP for Ebbw Vale since 1929, became its effective political director. Between them, Strauss and Bevan changed the political line, replacing Hartshorn with the independent-minded Raymond Postgate – until he and Bevan came to blows in 1941, when Bevan himself took on the title of editor, employing the former ILP journalist Jon Kimche as assistant editor to do the actual editing.

The post-Hartshorn *Tribune* was more-or-less in line with Orwell's politics, and he became an infrequent contributor under Postgate, though they fell out over a hostile Postgate review of *Betrayal of the Left* and Orwell subsequently dropped most of his left journalism work to concentrate on a job working in radio for the Eastern Service of the BBC, broadcasting highbrow cultural programmes and news analysis to India. Kimche's arrival made the *Tribune*-Orwell relationship much closer again: he was someone Orwell knew well (though it seems they did not like one another very much), having worked together in a Hampstead bookshop in the early 1930s and met again in Spain during the civil war, and was good friends with Tosco Fyvel, Orwell's collaborator on Searchlight Books in 1940-1941.

Orwell became a regular in the paper's pages in 1942-43, and when John Atkins, the literary editor, resigned in autumn 1943 to join Mass Observation, the organisation that pioneered the monitoring of public opinion in Britain, Fyvel lobbied Kimche to take on Orwell in his place. Kimche and Bevan agreed; Orwell was hired, starting in November 1943.

Tribune was not an official Labour publication in the 1940s and has never been one – though it has come close. But it was very firmly in the Labour camp when Orwell joined its staff and throughout his association with it. It took its own independent line and was willing to criticise the party leadership (which it did regularly) but its goal under Bevan's direction was unambiguously to agitate for a Labour government at the next general election – the date of which was unknown but assumed to be soon after the war's end. With the wartime coalition, Bevan had become the *de facto* one-man leader of the opposition and a media star – and in *Tribune* he had his pulpit, writing a column most weeks, dictating the editorial line (for the front of the paper at least) and dominating discussions about

PAUL ANDERSON

commissioning. Although Orwell was as literary editor between 1943 and 1945 in charge of the 'back half' of the paper, towards which Bevan took a hands-off approach, and although the column he wrote for *Tribune* between 1943 and 1947 (mostly under the rubric 'As I Please') deliberately steered clear of the stuff of everyday politics, his joining the paper marked his joining the Labour tribe.

It is true, as Newsinger argues in *Orwell's Politics*, that it is questionable how far Orwell embraced left Labour reformism even as he joined *Tribune*. Orwell's political thinking was influenced by several different left traditions, only partly shared with Bevan and most of the Labour left. In particular, Orwell was still engaged with the dissident libertarian and Trotskyist anti-Stalinist revolutionary socialist left that was obsessed with the degeneration of the Bolshevik revolution, the influence of which is apparent not only in his journalism but also in *Animal Farm* and *Nineteen Eighty-Four*. He was not fundamentally a parliamentary socialist: in spring 1944 he told the readers of *Partisan Review*: 'As a legislative body parliament has become relatively unimportant, and it has even less control over the executive than over the government. But it still functions as a kind of uncensored supplement to the radio – which, after all, is something worth preserving' (Orwell 1998 [1944]).

Nor was he optimistic about Labour's electoral prospects before 1945. Unlike Bevan, who in 1944-45 was insistent that the tide of public opinion was running to the left and that Labour would win a famous general election victory if only it broke with the coalition, Orwell took the view that because of the 'weakness of the Labour leaders' the party probably wouldn't break with the coalition and, even if it did, it would not make a 'serious effort to win' the general election (ibid). 'I have predicted all along that the Conservatives will win with a small majority,' declared Orwell just before Labour won a massive landslide (Orwell 1998 [1945a]).

But all this is compatible with Bernard Crick's description of Orwell's 1940s political stance as '*Tribune* socialism' (Crick 1980). Socialism might not be 'what Labour governments do', in Herbert Morrison's immortal phrase, but '*Tribune* socialism' was never more or less than what the paper has done. Orwell, as literary editor for 15 months, during which time he controlled a third of *Tribune*'s pages and occupied its most prominent bylined space, defined *Tribune* almost as much as Bevan. The wartime *Tribune* was a far more eclectic and open paper than it had been in its first three years and far less attached to left Labour parliamentary socialism than it became after 1945. As George Woodcock put it, '*Tribune* gave space, particularly in its literary pages, to many writers far closer in their views to the independent attitudes of the anarchists, Trotskyists and Independent Labour Party than they were to the policy of the official Labour Party' (Woodcock 1953). Orwell was by no means the only revolutionary or former revolutionary far-leftist who found a berth there. Others included the editor who first commissioned Orwell to write for the paper, Postgate; Orwell's contemporaries on the journalistic staff when he was literary editor, Kimche and Evelyn Anderson; his successor as literary editor, Fyvel; and, among contributors, Arthur Koestler, Tom Wintringham, Hugh Slater, Franz Borkenau, Reg Reynolds, Alex Comfort and Herbert Read.

The paper was in the mid-1940s at the height of its circulation, shifting 40,000 copies a week (about half the circulation of the rival *New Statesman*), and at the height of its prestige, a must-read paper for the political class and literary-cultural intellectuals as well as Labour activists. The circulation, boosted in part by wartime paper rationing, which limited the space available for comment and reviews in the daily and Sunday press, was sufficient to keep the paper afloat without too much help from Strauss's pockets (though Strauss supplied it with an almost-Fleet-Street office on the Strand, and he held editorial meetings at his millionaire pad next to Hyde Park). In Bevan, it had the most effective journalist-politician of his generation – and when he joined the cabinet in 1945 with responsibility for health and housing, his replacement as hands-on political director of *Tribune* was the most effective journalist-politician of the next generation, Michael Foot, a protégé of both Cripps and Bevan who had been elected in the 1945 Labour general election landslide as MP for Plymouth Devonport (and was already, in his early 30s, a former Fleet Street editor and noted controversialist left columnist and pamphleteer).

Bevan liked Orwell a lot, and the feeling was reciprocated, though they never became close. In October 1945, Orwell wrote a profile of Bevan anonymously for the *Observer*:

> Bevan thinks and feels as a working man. He knows how the scales are weighted against anyone with less than £5 a week. ... But he is remarkably free – some of his adversaries would say dangerously free – from any feeling of personal grievance against society. He shows no sign of ordinary class consciousness. He seems equally at home in all kinds of company. It is difficult to imagine anyone less impressed by social status or less inclined to put on airs with subordinates. ... He does not have the suspicion of 'cleverness' and anaesthesia to the arts which are generally regarded as the mark of a practical man. Those who have worked with him in a journalistic capacity have remarked with pleasure and astonishment that here at last is a politician who knows that literature exists and will even hold up work for five minutes to discuss a point of style (Orwell 1998 [1945b]).

Orwell's relationship with Foot was more distant – as a columnist from 1945 Orwell was not part of the staff and they disagreed on

PAUL ANDERSON

several key issues of foreign policy as the Cold War got under way, most importantly the 1947 pamphlet by Foot, Richard Crossman and Ian Mikardo, *Keep Left*, demanding a 'third way' foreign policy for Britain (neither pro-American nor pro-Soviet), which Orwell thought naïve, and Foot's late-1940s enthusiasm, shared by just about all of Orwell's *Tribune* friends, for a Jewish state in Palestine.

THE 1945 LABOUR GOVERNMENT

But this is to get ahead of events. Through *Tribune*, Orwell joined the Labour tribe, but he never joined the Labour Party, as far as we know, and Orwell left *Tribune* as an employee in spring 1945 to become a foreign correspondent for the *Observer*, well before the 1945 UK general election or indeed the end of the war – though he was to return as a freelance columnist. The *Observer* job did not last long: his wife Eileen died after a botched operation, and he came back to London in late spring 1945, utterly emotionally devastated, just before the defeat of Germany and the subsequent election, and just before publication of *Animal Farm*. There is no doubt that Orwell supported Labour in 1945 and no doubt that he covered the campaign as a journalist – and he might even have canvassed for Labour, a story that many biographers tell but of which there is no evidence beyond the anecdotal.

But what did he think of the Labour government? He was writing for *Tribune* – he took up the column again in autumn 1945, which he kept up until May 1947. But to what extent was he signed up for the whole Labour package?

In a 'London Letter' to *Partisan Review*, written just after the election, Orwell was ambiguous: 'One cannot take this slide to the left as meaning that Britain is on the verge of revolution,' he declares. 'The mood of the country seems less revolutionary, less utopian, even less hopeful than it was in 1940 or 1942.' But:

> A Labour government may be said to mean business if it (a) nationalises land, coal mines, railways, public utilities and banks, (b) offers India immediate dominion status (this is a minimum), and (c) purges the bureaucracy, the army, the diplomatic service etc, so thoroughly as to forestall sabotage from the right… If these don't happen, it is good bet that no really radical economic change is intended (Orwell 1998 [1945a]).

Orwell warns that the next few years will be tough because voters had not been warned of the austerity that would inevitably accompany war reconstruction and the end of colonialism. But, he goes on:

> The new government starts off in a very strong position. Unless the party suffers a serious split, Labour is secure in office for five

years, probably longer. ... The people who are in power this time are not a gang of easily-bribed weaklings like those of 1929 (ibid).

He is dismissive of Attlee – who lacks 'the magnetism that a statesman needs nowadays' – but 'the other people in a commanding position in the government, Bevin, Morrison, Greenwood, Cripps, Aneurin Bevan, are tougher and abler than their opposite numbers in the Conservative Party' (Orwell 1998 [1945b]). In an essay in *Commentary* in late 1945 he declared that 'the Labour government has at least five years in hand, and the men at the top of it, as a body, are at least as able and determined as any government we have had for decades past. It is too early to cheer, but a hopeful attitude is justified' (Orwell 1998 [1945c]). His main worries in 1945-46 were that the government was insufficiently committed to maintaining civil liberties and was not moving quickly enough to introduce socialism. 'Even allowing for the fact that everything takes time,' he wrote in *Partisan Review* in 1946:

> ... it is astonishing how little change seems to have happened in the structure of society. In a purely economic sense, I suppose, the drift is towards socialism, or at least state ownership. ... But in the social set-up there is no symptom by which one could infer that we are not living under a Conservative government. No move has been made against the House of Lords, for example, there has been no talk of disestablishing the Church, there has been very little replacement of Tory ambassadors, service chiefs or other high officials, and if any effort is really being made to democratise education, it has borne no fruit as yet. ... I think almost any observer would have expected a greater change in the social atmosphere when a Labour government with a crushing majority had been in power for eight months (Orwell 1998 [1946b]).

Orwell's sense of disappointment with Labour's failure to shift the mood of the nation, shared with every *Tribune* writer, never left him – but nor did his support for the Attlee government's broad programme. And in one respect, on foreign policy, he was more pro-government than almost anyone else on the paper. On the biggest contested international issues of the day – the emerging Cold War and the future of Palestine – Orwell supported Ernest Bevin as foreign secretary against Foot, Bevan and their closest comrades on *Tribune*. He argued from early on that there was no alternative to a military alliance between America and the western European democracies against the Soviet Union and that in Palestine Bevin was right to resist the creation of a Jewish nation-state that dispossessed the Arab population. He also took a particularly hard line against communist fellow-travellers in the Labour Party, though little of it was published in his lifetime.

He remained a regular reader of the paper, referred favourably to it in print on a couple of occasions and stayed on good personal terms with his *Tribune* friends Evelyn Anderson and Fyvel, with whom he kept up a frequent correspondence. He asked Fyvel to remember him to 'everyone at the office' in December 1948, and when, on the publication of *Nineteen Eighty-Four* in June 1949, the paper ran a short item wishing him a speedy recovery asked Fyvel to 'thank the others at *Tribune* for putting in such a kind par'.

But Orwell was not really an active player in the political world of the late 1940s. He decided to move out of London in May 1946, to an almost ridiculously isolated farmhouse on the Scottish island of Jura, and spent most of the rest of his life there, increasingly disabled by his tuberculosis, writing the novel that became *Nineteen Eighty-Four*. Whenever he left Jura after 1947 it was for sanitoriums: after two years of enjoying life in one of the most beautiful remote locations in the world, he became terminally ill and died.

CONCLUSION

The argument about Orwell's relationship with Labour is not over. But the idea that he was anything other than a democratic socialist for all of his life as a public intellectual is nonsense. He was not at any point an orthodox Labourite and was always sceptical about the Labour Party even though he supported it in the 1940s. But that is a position shared, rightly or wrongly, by many others in his own time and since.

REFERENCES

Anderson, Paul (2015) In defence of Bernard Crick, Keeble, Richard L. (ed.) *George Orwell Now!*, New York: Peter Lang pp 83-98

Anderson, Paul (2006) Introduction, Anderson, Paul (ed.) *Orwell In* Tribune*: 'As I Please' and Other Writings*, London: Methuen pp 1-56

'Cato' (1940) (Foot, Michael, Owen, Frank and Howard, Peter), *Guilty Men*, London: Gollancz

Colls, Robert (2013) *George Orwell: English Rebel*, Oxford: OUP

Crick, Bernard (1982) *George Orwell: A Life*, Harmondsworth: Penguin

Labedz, Leopold (1984) Will George Orwell survive until 1984?, *Encounter*, June/July-August

Orwell, George (1998 [1937]), *The Road to Wigan Pier* Davison, Peter (ed.) *CWGO*, London: Secker and Warburg, Vol. 5, chapter 11

Orwell, George (1998 [1938]) Why I join the ILP, *CWGO*, Vol 11 pp 167-169; *New Leader*, 24 June

Orwell, George (1998 [1940]) 'The Home Guard and you', *CWGO*, Vol 12 pp 309-312, *Tribune*, 20 December

Orwell, George (1998 [1941a]) *The Lion and the Unicorn: Socialism and the English Genius*, *CWGO*, Vol 12 pp 391-432; London: Searchlight Books

Orwell, George (1998 [1941b]) Patriots and Revolutionaries, *Betrayal of the Left*, *CWGO*, Vol. 12 pp 343-350

Orwell, George (1998 [1942a]) London Letter, *Partisan Review*, July-August, *CWGO*, Vol. 13 pp 302-309

Orwell, George (1998 [1942b]) BBC weekly news review for India, 14 March, *CWGO*, Vol. 13 pp 224-227

Orwell, George (1998 [1942c]) Wartime diary, 7 June, *CWGO*, Vol. 13 p. 351

Orwell, George (1998 [1942d]) Wartime diary, 10 August, *CWGO*, Vol. 12 p. 438

Orwell, George (1998 [1944]) London Letter, *Partisan Review*, Spring, *CWGO*, Vol. 16 pp 64-70

Orwell, George (1998 [1945a]) London Letter. *Partisan Review*, Summer, *CWGO*, Vol. 16 pp 161-165

Orwell. George (1998 [1945b]) 'Nye Bevan'. *Observer*, 14 October, *CWGO*, Vol. 16 pp 310-313

Orwell, George (1998 [1946a]) Why I Write, *CWGO*, Vol. 18 pp 316-322; *Gangrel*, Summer

Orwell, George (1998 [1946b]) London Letter, *Partisan Review*, Summer, *CWGO*, Vol. 19 pp 285-289

Newsinger, John (1999) *Orwell's Politics*, Basingstoke: Macmillan

Pimlott, Ben (1977) *Labour and the Left in the 1930s*, Cambridge: Cambridge University Press

Wilkin, Pete (2013) George Orwell: The English Dissident as Tory Anarchist, *Political Studies*, Vol. 61, No. 1 pp 197-214

Woodcock, George (1953) *The Crystal Spirit: A Study of George Orwell*, Boston: Little Brown

NOTE ON THE CONTRIBUTOR

Paul Anderson was reviews editor of *Tribune* (1986-1991) its editor (1991-1993), then deputy editor of the *New Statesman* (1993-1996). He currently teaches journalism at the University of Essex.

PAPER

The Orwell Conundrum in *Coming Up for Air*: A Call for Action or Passive Resistance?

ORIOL QUINTANA

Among the many ways Orwell's novel Coming Up for Air *(1939) has been read, two different interpretations stand out in clear contrast: the novel is understood as a call for action, a preparation for the revolution, or alternatively, it is considered an exploration of powerlessness and passive resistance. This paper aims at showing that both interpretations have solid biographical and textual grounds (hence the 'conundrum'), but argues that the second has become more relevant in the face of the present-day development of the technological society.*

Keywords: Orwell, *Coming Up for Air*, technological society, twenty-first century, humanism

THE ORWELL CONUNDRUM IN *COMING UP FOR AIR*

In 1992, Erika Gottlieb published her *The Orwell Conundrum: A Cry of Despair or Faith in the Spirit of Man?* She argued that Orwell, in *Nineteen Eighty-Four*, wanted to make a case for the human spirit, trying to build a twentieth-century humanism, 'an affirmation of moral-spiritual values that does not follow from faith in religion but from a deep-seated faith in the spirit of Man' (Gottlieb 1992: 19). Gottlieb's book was necessary because a few influential critics had described the novel as a product of despair. One of them was Orwell's publisher Fredric Warburg, whose famous report on *Nineteen Eighty-Four* began: 'This is amongst the most terrifying books I have ever read,' and ended with: 'It is a great book, but I pray I may be spared from reading another like it for years to come' (Meyers 1975: 247, 250). Gottlieb's book, written decades after the first edition of the novel, had the necessary balance and detachment to offer an alternative, deeper reading, and it argued that Orwell really believed in man, even if he chose to write a terrifying book on his destruction.

Coming Up For Air opens up similar dilemmas. In the novel, George Bowling has gone to Lower Binfield, the place where he was born and spent his childhood, hoping to rekindle the intensity of feeling, the calmness and some of the simplicity of life of his childhood years. Bowling is exhausted, emptied of all 'vital juice' by a meaningless job, an unloved and unloving wife and two annoying children. He feels that his life conditions are a prison – a car, and a semi-detached house in a London suburb – although from a certain point of view he is 'a success' having risen from his humble origins. But he can find no rest, especially at the time when war was threatening.

By going to Lower Binfield, he has tried to 'come up for air'. He has planned the escape in secrecy, playing truant to his wife who would never understand nor approve of his trip. But to his dismay, Bowling discovers that Lower Binfield has been engulfed in the general tendency of the time: it has become much like the suburb Bowling was living in. The pond where he had fished as a child has been transformed into a dumping ground. The trip has proved an utter failure and Bowling has clearly made a fool of himself. Is it really worth trying to make his wife understand, in the face of the false accusation of his having had an affair during his outing, or would such efforts simply lead to more ridicule?

In a certain sense, Orwell is asking the reader to complete the story, to answer the riddle: the modern world is becoming increasingly a prison, and a prison we seem happy to build from the inside. Should we take action to change this current or should we just try to endure it? The novel clearly suggests, through the Bowling character and the story's ending, that it is possible to 'stay human' – which Winston Smith is not able to do at the end of *Nineteen Eighty-Four*.

A CALL FOR ACTION?

In 1980, when Bernard Crick's biography was published, the novel was already being read as a call for action (Crick 1992 [1980]: 376). It made perfect sense. After going through two momentous life experiences, as a committed reporter in Wigan and as a militiaman in Spain, Orwell had finally clarified his political stance. In *The Road to Wigan Pier* (1937), Orwell had defended the idea that socialists had to win the support of the middle class, the new class of 'office-workers and black-coated employees' (*CWGO* 5: 210), since 'Socialism, in the form in which it is now presented, appeals chiefly to unsatisfactory or even inhuman types' (ibid: 169), and because 'we are at a moment when it is desperately necessary for left-wingers of all complexions to drop their differences and hang together' (ibid: 205). Therefore, it was just 'fatal to let the ordinary inquirer get away with the idea that being a Socialist means wearing sandals and burbling about dialectical materialism' (ibid: 208). On the contrary, Socialists should try to attract the 'office-worker type', like George Bowling, because 'all these people have the same interests and the same enemies as the working class. All are being robbed and bullied by the same system' (ibid: 210).

It was urgent to win over the sinking middle class, 'the private schoolmaster, the half-starved free-lance journalist, the colonel's spinster daughter with £75 a year, the jobless Cambridge graduate, the ship's officer without a ship, the clerks, the civil servants, the commercial travellers, and the thrice-bankrupt drapers in country towns' (ibid: 215). *Coming Up for Air* features such a member of the 'sinking middle class' – one who is being 'robbed and bullied' by the system. In his reflections, Bowling realises that 'nine-tenths of the people in Ellesmere Road are under the impression that they own their houses' (*CWGO* 7: 11), when in fact, the houses are on lease-hold and they will never be the owners; building societies extract a huge profit by controlling all the construction process and the lease-holders pay a few times the value they get. And what is worse, they become 'yes-men and bumsuckers', in the fiction of being 'respectable householders' (ibid: 13).

The new urban developments were a sort of swindle, Ellesmere Road being 'just a prison with the cells in a row. A line of semi-detached torture-chambers where the poor little five-to-ten-pound-a-weekers quake and shiver…' (ibid: 10), afraid of losing their job, under the pressure of supporting a wife and children. Bowling insists, after entering a store and witnessing how a floor-manager was publicly scolding one of the clerks, that people like these were just frightened: 'Everyone that isn't scared stiff of losing his job is scared stiff of war, or Fascism, or Communism, or something' (ibid: 15-16). Life for the middle class, was, despite external appearances, as precarious and unsatisfactory as for the working class. As soon as Bowling starts remembering his life as a child, it becomes obvious to him, and to anyone reading the novel, that the modern world is not able to provide for anyone's non-material necessities.

In comparison, life was much more satisfying and full at the beginning of the twentieth century, before the First World War: before the general spread of technology and the consumer mind-set emerged (suggested in the novel by the references to gramophones, milk-bars, tea-shops, stockings factories, and the extension of urban life-styles). In the possible case of a revolutionary government establishing itself in England, the middle classes should clearly support it, as they had really nothing to lose, and thus they could even have a say in the way industrial development was changing the world, acting as a 'sort of permanent opposition' (*CWGO* 5: 204) to the excesses of the technological society.

Despite having gone through political persecution, Orwell ended his Spanish experience stating: 'Curiously enough, the whole experience has left me with not less but more belief in the decency of human beings' (*CWGO* 6: 186), which suggests that he believed that political appeals, writings and actions were still worth the effort. In the first days in Catalonia, Orwell had seen a revolution in progress, and even if he later wrote 'all revolutions are failures....' (*CWGO 16*: 400) those images were deeply settled in his heart, in a way that led him to believe that even the Local Defence Volunteers, the Home Guard, which he joined in 1940 (Meyers 2000: 199), were not so different from the Catalan militia. They were, therefore, an opportunity for the English people to seize power: 'People dimly grasped – and not always so dimly, to judge from certain conversations I listened to in pubs at the time – that it was our duty both to defend England and to turn it into a genuine democracy' (*CWGO* 12: 345).

Orwell never stopped being a rebel, and *Coming up for Air* is consistent with his rebellious trend. Only one minor detail could refute this general interpretation. In December 1937, when he was in a sanatorium in Aylesford, Kent, recovering from a new outbreak of his lung disease, he described *Coming up for Air* to Leonard Moore, his literary agent, thus (*CWGO* 11: 100):

> I am glad Mr Gollancz is already showing much solicitude about my next book, but I have only a vague idea of it as yet, as you may well imagine. All I have thought of it is: it will be a novel, *it will not be about politics*, and it will be about a man who is having a holiday and trying to make a temporary escape from his responsibilities, public and private. The title I thought of is 'Coming Up For Air' ... (my italics).

At that point, the book was just a vague idea, but it would seem that from the moment Orwell set pen to paper, the prospect of not writing about politics faded away. Orwell wrote the novel in Morocco, where he and his first wife Eileen had gone at the expense of the novelist L. H. Myers (1881-1944), who anonymously provided the money for their stay. They departed from England on the third of December, 1938, and during the six months they spent in Africa, the possibility of the outbreak of war came closer. Some letters of Eileen Blair (Shelden 1991: 302) bear testimony that the Orwells were deeply concerned over the future, and that Orwell's principal terrors were 'the concentration camp and the famine'. Orwell wrote to his long-time friend Cyril Connolly confessing: 'Everything one writes now is overshadowed by this ghastly feeling that we are rushing towards a precipice and, though we shan't actually prevent ourselves or anyone from going over, must put up some sort of fight' (*CWGO* 11: 253).

Coming Up for Air is a warning about the post-war situation, rather than a warning about the war itself. Orwell believed that, after or even during the war, some sort of fascist regime would be established

ORIOL QUINTANA

in England, and thought people were hardly aware of what that meant. His Spanish experience had left him fearing wars and totalitarian regimes, so he felt it necessary to impress upon people the awfulness of both. George Bowling reflects on the prospect of both possibilities throughout the novel (for instance, *CWGO* 7: 21, 26, 153, 157, 167, 174). A particular passage is reminiscent of the last paragraph of *Homage to Catalonia*, his personal account of fighting on the Republican side during the Spanish civil war (1938). In the moment an R. A. F. aircraft accidentally drops a bomb over Lower Binfield, Bowling reflects (*CWGO* 7, 233):

> ...I had time to think that there's something grand about the bursting of a big projectile ... the peculiar thing is the feeling it gives you of being suddenly shoved up against reality. It's like being woken up by somebody shying a bucket of water over you. You're suddenly dragged out of your dreams by a clang of bursting metal, and it's terrible, and it's real.

Just as *Homage to Catalonia*'s ending incorporated a denunciation of the 'deep, deep sleep of England', *Coming Up for Air* also tried to make the English people aware of the necessity of fighting fascism, and to oppose a war that would be its first stage. Orwell was certainly for putting up 'some sort of fight' with his novel. Meyers (2000: 193) also refers to Orwell's wartime journalism to further prove this point: 'Though the novel is full of yearning for the past, Orwell was intellectually convinced of the need for a revolution, and his wartime journalism looked forward to the radical changes that would be made by a Socialist government.' Rodden and Rossi (2012: 19, 23, 26) also support this reading. After all, it was Orwell himself who, in *The Lion and the Unicorn* (1941), advocated the coming together of working and middle class (*CWGO* 12: 421) 'If it can be made clear that defeating Hitler means wiping out class privilege,' then 'the great mass of middling people, the 6 pounds a week to 2000 a year class, will probably be on our side.'

For Saunders (2016: 17) 'Bowling is the stuff revolutions are made of'. While Wykes (1987: 106) argues that Hilda will believe for ever that George has been with a woman, and that the love affair he has attempted is, essentially, 'with his boyhood past and it has proved impossible to realize'. Saunders goes on to claim that the ending of the novel has to be read as if Bowling is actually going to take action, *and* try to make his wife understand.

The three options Bowling set for himself were (*CWGO* 7: 247):

> A. To tell her what I'd really been doing and somehow make her believe me.

> B. To pull the old gag about losing my memory.

C. To let her go on thinking it was a woman, and take my medicine.

But, damn it! I knew which it would have to be.

According to Saunders, since 'there could be no sensible use of an exclamation mark indicative of resignation', the last sentence of the novel had to be read: 'Damn it, I will make my wife understand me!' (Saunders 2016: 105). The 'damn it!', with an exclamation mark, represents Bowling's reaction against himself, because just a few lines earlier, he has assumed that there was 'no use playing injured innocence any longer', claiming 'All I wanted was the line of least resistance' (*CWGO* 7: 247). This would indicate that, although at first he was going to let his wife believe he had had an affair, at the very last moment he changed his mind.

OR IS *COMING UP FOR AIR* A CALL FOR PASSIVE RESISTANCE?

There is strong textual evidence that Orwell, through *Coming Up for Air*, was again trying to convey a sense of powerlessness. After all, 'The sense of powerlessness is a central theme in all six of Orwell's major works of fiction' (Van Dellen 1975: 58). The main characters of *Keep the Aspidistra Flying*, *A Clergyman's Daughter* and *Coming Up for Air* have no other choice but to *come around*, in a circular movement, to do what was expected of them, after an attempt to find some authenticity – as Michel Carter (1985) argues. The main characters in those three novels have more in common than Flory and Smith in *Burmese Days* and *Nineteen Eighty-Four*, who do not survive their attempts at rebellion: they can find no way to resist what society imposes on them, and they end up physically or spiritually dead.

The suspicion of bad faith, of inauthenticity, floats over Dorothy Hare (of *The Clergyman's Daughter*) and Gordon Comstock (of *Keep the Aspidistra Flying*), but not over Bowling. That's what makes him a more solid character and *Coming Up for Air* a better novel than its forerunners: it is as if Orwell, in his previous novels, had been investigating the terms of a pact with an unsatisfactory, dehumanising world, and only in *Coming Up for Air* had he found an acceptable compromise. The compromise works like this: Bowling (by not trying to explain himself to his wife) will accept his wife's reprimand, and with it, a marriage that's a trap; he will accept a world of tinned food, money worship, rotten landscapes and the prospect of war if it he must; and in exchange for all of that, he will be allowed to remain human *because he will not be forced to love any of these things*.

What Bowling learns throughout the novel is how solid and well-founded are his motives for rejecting the modern world, but also that he is allowed to keep his love for the things the world officially forbids. The world only demands an apparent, external submission, but allows the individual to remain faithful to what is really valuable. This passive resistance had been foreshadowed by Comstock's reflections (*CWGO* 4: 268):

> Our civilization is founded on greed and fear, but in the lives of common men the greed and fear are mysteriously transmuted into something nobler. The lower-middle-class people were there, behind their lace curtains, with their children and their scraps of furniture and their aspidistras – they lived by the money-code, sure enough, and yet they contrived to keep their decency. ... They had their standards, their inviolable points of honour. They kept themselves 'respectable' – kept the aspidistra flying.

Since the passage contains the expression 'keep the aspidistra flying', which gives the book its title, one has to assume that the paragraph sums up the point Orwell was trying to make with the novel. A point that only appears in the end after an unexpected turn of events (Rosemary, Comstock's girlfriend, becomes pregnant). It is exactly the same point one can read in Bowling's story, only that the idea appears right from the beginning, as soon as the reader gets familiar with Bowling's attitude to life: as much as his awareness of the deficiencies of his life conditions, he never falls into despair nor tries to embellish them by self-deception. Orwell was, in fact, exploring a way of coming to terms with a money-worshipping, dehumanised world, and formulated a 'right' way of being-in-the-world through Bowling's character.[1]

Those who have read *Coming Up for Air* as an optimistic work, despite its cul-de-sac ending, have focused, implicitly or overtly, on the fact that the individual's love for what is valuable will survive, even if for it to do so, the individual has to submit: 'the individual victim of this technocracy will survive only if he passively submits to it' (Van Dellen 1975: 63). Galván, for example (1989: 91), sees a connection between Bowling and the Italian militiaman Orwell celebrates at the start of *Homage to Catalonia*, in the sense that both keep a purity of spirit, a radical decency that consists in loving what is lovable against all odds, either in the midst of a war or in the midst of technocratic world. What else could a fat insurance salesman and a fierce soldier have in common?

Anette Federico also offers an optimistic reading of the novel and claims that Orwell is calling for a kind of 'mute disobedience' (2005: 54). For her, the novel is not defeatist nor apocalyptic – as Meyers argues (1975b) – but contains a number of strategies by which the individual can maintain an inconspicuous rebellion against society: 'blissful reading is a minor transgression in George's society, where "the idea of doing things because you enjoy them" is heretical' (Federico op cit: 57).

Just keeping up the memory of old times past is a private act of rebellion, so Brooker (2006) suggests. The nostalgia of the past that *Coming Up for Air* so powerfully conveys is neither futile nor merely sentimental: 'The past is a literary heritage, to be handled delicately: *but is also a political resource*' (my italics) (Brooker 2006: 295). To remember the past is to keep alive one's love for what is valuable, and a way of having a spiritual reservoir from where political action can spring when the opportunity arises.

Passive resistance is certainly denied by totalitarian governments and the stress on this in *Nineteen Eighty-Four* makes it such a terrifying novel. Bowling finds it difficult to express it, but he still loves beauty (although he can find no place nor time for fishing), righteousness (although his economic conditions compel him to be more of a 'yes-man' and a 'bum-sucker' than a revolutionary) and truth (although he cannot tell his true feelings to his wife. But he can see through the hatred of the Left Book Club speaker and through 'the swindle of progress').

Totalitarianism is the definitive threat to the love an individual can feel for truth, righteousness and beauty. In a fully-developed totalitarian regime *they* get inside you, there is no way of keeping an individual line of resistance, a crystal spirit, nor any form of decency. Any aspiration for truth, justice or beauty is substituted by the cult of might: 'Old Hitler's something different. So's Joe Stalin. They aren't like these chaps in the old days who crucified people and chopped their heads off and so forth, just for the fun of it. They're after something quite new – something that's never been heard of before' (*CWGO* 7: 165).[2]

Significantly, just after completing *Coming Up for Air*, Orwell published *Inside the Whale* (1940), further arguing in favour of passive resistance.[3] Henry Miller's works were a confession of impotence, and a frivolity, and precisely because of that, they were a better defence of humanity than other books with a clear political purpose. Miller's works were an implicit form of resistance.

Such a point sheds light on *Coming Up for Air* and the character of George Bowling. Bowling expresses, in different moments, a few doubts about his escape to Lower Binfield. He is perfectly aware that his outing is untimely, and he needs to conceal it. He feels it is an attack on the established order, a sort of minor revolution, just like his decision to pull aside his car to pick flowers in an earlier passage of the novel, before his decision to go back to Lower Binfield (*CWGO* 7: 172). These acts are frivolities that Bowling allows himself, and a part of him feels ashamed of them. They are private acts of resistance rather than sheer acts of irresponsibility, much as they might appear so from the outside. Just like the lives and wasted talents of Henry Miller's characters. As Orwell concluded on Miller (*CWGO* 12: 11):

ORIOL QUINTANA

> The passive attitude will come back, and it will be more consciously passive than before. Progress and reaction have both turned out to be swindles. Seemingly there is nothing left but quietism – robbing reality of its terrors by simply submitting to it. Get inside the whale – or rather, admit you are inside the whale (for you are, of course). Give yourself over to the world-process, stop fighting against it or pretending that you control it; simply accept it, endure it, record it.

He was trying to justify both the writings of an author who thought that 'progress and reaction' had revealed themselves as swindles, and his beloved George Bowling, who had to keep 'inside the whale', compelled to 'quietism' and to escape the terrors of reality by 'submitting to it'. *Coming up for Air*'s ending is an example of the submission that, despite appearances, is the right way of continuing the human heritage in times of collective lunacy.

TODAY'S RELEVANCE OF *COMING UP FOR AIR*

Political action and passive resistance are not mutually exclusive. There's a time for both. Whatever we choose to do, ours is a time in which the menace of technological totalitarianism has surpassed the menace of political totalitarianism. This fact is implicit in the critical study of Van Dellen (1975), in which he quotes Ellul (1912-1994), a French thinker and author of *The Technological Society* (1964) who denounced the de-humanisation of man under technology.

According to Ellul (ibid: 376), the common man, in leaving his workplace 'his joy in finishing his stint is mixed with dissatisfaction with work as fruitless as it is incomprehensible and as far from really productive work'. This is strongly reminiscent of Bowling's admission that the assurance business is a kind of open swindle (*CWGO* 7: 13): 'My own line, insurance, is a swindle I admit, but it's an open swindle with the cards on the table.'

Coming up for Air can, then, be taken as a reference work for anyone who studies the present-day development of technological society. Just as *Nineteen Eighty-Four* was and is still *the* reference for studying how totalitarian societies operate and can be considered a compendium of the terrors of the twentieth century, *Coming Up for Air* is best seen as Orwell's warning on many of the horrors of the twenty-first century.

NOTES

[1] Van Dellen claimed that Orwell could not resolve the dilemma of powerlessness (Van Dellen 1975: 56), but at the same time, stressed that Bowling 'passively submits to the modern world, but his submission not only means endurance, *it means the ultimate victory of man's basic humanity* '(p. 66). So, after all, maybe Orwell did resolve the dilemma of powerlessness

² German philosopher Byung-Chul Han in *Der Freundlicher Big Brother* (*The Friendly Big Brother*) argues that social control today is much more effective than in totalitarian regimes of the past (Han 2015: 53-57)

³ Cf. Alfred Pérles' account of the encounter of Miller and Orwell, in *Orwell Remembered* (Coppard and Crick, London: Ariel Books/BBC, 1989 pp 216-219)

REFERENCES

Brooker, Joseph (2006) Forbidden to dream again: Orwell and nostalgia, *English,* Vol. 55 pp 213, 281-297

Carter, Michael (1985) *George Orwell and the Problem of Authentic Existence,* Totowa, New Jersey: Barnes and Noble Books

Coppard, Audrey and Crick, Bernard (eds) (1989) *Memoria y evocación de George Orwell*, Mexico: Fondo de Cultura Económica, Mexican edition of *Orwell Remembered*

Crick, Bernard (1992 [1980]) *George Orwell: A life*, London: Penguin, third edition

Davison, Peter (ed.) (1998) *The Complete Works of George Orwell*, 20 Vols, London: Secker and Warburg

Ellul, Jacques (1964) *The Technological Society*, New York: Vintage Books

Federico, Annette (2005) Making do: George Orwell's *Coming Up for Air, Studies in the Novel*, Vol. 37, No. 1, Spring pp 50-63

Galván, Fernando (1989) Reading *Coming Up For Air* and *Nineteen Eighty-Four* in the light of Orwell's Spanish experience, *Bells: Barcelona English Language and Literature Studies*, Vol. 1 pp 87-92

Gottlieb, Erika (1992) *The Orwell Conundrum: A Cry of Despair or 'Faith in the Spirit of Man?'*, Ottawa: Carleton University Press

Han, Byung-Chul (2015) *Psychopolitik: Neoliberalismus und die neuen Machttechniken* [*Psychopolitics: Neo-liberalism and the New Power Techniques*], Frankfurt am Main: S. Fischer, fifth edition

Meyers, Jeffrey (1975) *George Orwell: The Critical Heritage*, London: Routledge and Kegan Paul

Meyers, Jeffrey (1975b) Orwell's apocalypse: *Coming Up for Air, Modern Fiction Studies*, Vol. 21, No. 1, Spring pp 69-80

Meyers, Jeffrey (2000) *Orwell: The Wintry Conscience of a Generation*, New York: W. W. Norton

Rodden, John (ed.) (2012) *The Cambridge Introduction to George Orwell*, New York: Cambridge University Press

Saunders, Loraine (2016) *The Unsung Artistry of George Orwell: The Novels from Burmese Days to Nineteen Eighty-Four*, London: Taylor and Francis, Kindle Edition

Shelden, Michael (1991) *Orwell: The Authorized Biography*. New York: HarperCollins

Van Dellen, Robert J. (1975) George Orwell's *Coming Up for Air*: The politics of powerlessness, *Modern Fiction Studies*, Vol. 21, No. 1 pp 57-68

Wykes, David (1987) *A Preface to George Orwell*, London: Longman

NOTE ON THE CONTRIBUTOR

Oriol Quintana teaches Ethics at IQS-URL in Barcelona (oriol.quintana@iqs.url.edu).

Death, Hegemony and Masks: Reimaging Theories of Resistance Through the Writings of George Orwell

HARRY BARK

The recent publication of George Orwell: The Collected Poetry *has enabled a new focus on an area of Orwell's work that is often overlooked. Many of Orwell's early novels have been similarly marginalised, not least by Orwell himself, in a manner that disassociates them from his later writing. Through the theoretical framework of resistance, defined through the work of Antonio Gramsci and James Scott, this paper demonstrates how a selection of Orwell's poems published in* The Adelphi *between 1933 and 1934 and his early novel* Keep the Aspidistra Flying *(1936) can be re-evaluated as part of a developmental process that culminates in* Nineteen Eighty-Four *(1949).*

Keywords: resistance, masks, *The Adelphi*, *Keep the Aspidistra Flying*, *Nineteen Eighty-Four*

APPROACHES TO ORWELL AND RESISTANCE

A general critical consensus on the writings of George Orwell positions his novels and poetry of the 1930s as forgettable in relation to the later works of *Animal Farm* (1945) and *Nineteen Eighty-Four* (1949). Orwell's own correspondence seems to support this. In a letter to George Woodcock in 1946, he claims that at the time of writing *Keep the Aspidistra Flying* (1936): 'I simply hadn't a book in me' and the novel was one of a number of his works that he was 'ashamed of and have not allowed to be reprinted' (Orwell 1970: 241). In a later letter, he dismisses the novel as a 'silly potboiler' (*CWGO* 17: 114). However, recent approaches to Orwell have reconsidered such dismissals. John Rodden and John Rossi suggest *Keep the Aspidistra Flying* is better than Orwell's 'silly potboiler' condemnation (Rodden and Rossi 2012: 41), whilst Ben Clarke argues that the novel 'demonstrates the evolution of his critical method' (Clarke 2015: 545). This suggestion is significant in terms of the academic field of Orwell studies as it seeks to connect his critically and popularly acclaimed works with the lesser known and often discredited texts. In addition, it attempts to create an understanding of Orwell as a long-developing writer rather than presenting him as a writer who experiences an unexpectedly powerful literary upturn in the final years of his life.

Clarke's claim that *Keep the Aspidistra Flying* holds a clear connection to Orwell's later work can be further extended to incorporate his poetry. It is notable that in critical guides and companions to Orwell his poetry is relatively unexamined and often entirely ignored. Despite Rodden and Rossi's claims regarding *Keep the Aspidistra Flying* in the Cambridge guides (*The Cambridge Companion to George* Orwell, of 2007, and *The Cambridge Introduction to George Orwell*, of 2012), their defence of Orwell's earlier work does not extend to his poetry. It is only recently that a collected works of Orwell's poetry has been published and the editorial analysis given in *George Orwell: The Complete Poetry* (2015) is largely biographical, providing a rather limited approach to this area of Orwell's work. Analysis of the poetry that is rooted in critical engagement as opposed to biographical interpretation offers scope for new readings that view Orwell's later work as founded in his early projects.

READING ORWELL THROUGH SCOTT AND GRAMSCI

Orwell's poetic output is heavily weighted towards his juvenilia, yet a small number of poems published in *The Adelphi* between March 1933 and April 1934 are essential in understanding the developing conceptual attitude of Orwell's work. The reimaging of *Nineteen Eighty-Four* through analysis of *Keep the Aspidistra Flying* and *The Adelphi* poems, a selection of which will be considered in this paper, gives scope for seeing these texts as a literary space in which to explore theories of resistance. Orwell's dystopian final novel has resistance at its core as Winston and Julia attempt to undermine the Party through their insubordinate actions. Indeed, their failed rebellion, which serves to reaffirm the extensive dominance of the Party, can be usefully considered in relation to the notions of resistance and hegemony of Antonio Gramsci and James Scott.

Scott theorises the forms of resistance available to groups who are subject to domination by focusing on communities that do not have the capacity to revolt or overtly resist. A pragmatic insubordination within relations of domination emerges as the most effective manner of resistance. Scott argues that for the dominated groups this is the only form of resistance available since open insubordination 'in almost any context will provoke a more rapid and ferocious reaction than an insubordination that … never ventures to contest the formal definitions of hierarchy and power' (Scott 2002 [1985]: 93). This sets the essential choice of resistance for Scott between a suicidal overt rebellion that is destined to end in defeat and retribution, or a resistance that has a limited, yet prolonged, potential.

For Gramsci, the hegemony of a ruling group assimilates any insubordinate who is forced to conform publicly to the values of the ruling body (Gramsci 2002 [1971]: 67). Accordingly, the authority of a dominating body lies essentially in their hegemonic social and moral discourse. The dominant group has access to institutions of influence, such as schools and the media, leading to a social discourse of 'common sense' which places groups as naturally in their position of subordination (ibid). John Hoffman explains that the hegemonic role of a dominating class is not only to maintain power but to win 'active support' (Hoffman 1984: 74). Consequently, a group that adopts dominant values, even out of necessity, normalises hegemonic values. Whilst Scott suggests that insubordinates act out conformity as a performance of their weakness, Gramsci argues that the cultural monopoly of a dominant group can overwhelm the resistant character of that act. Although Gramsci ultimately offers a revolutionary theorisation of hegemony by suggesting that a counter-hegemonic consciousness can develop in the resistant group to eventually form their own hegemony, his theory can be reimagined through Orwell's narratives of dominance.

Whether through the totalitarian structures of Airstrip One in *Nineteen Eighty-Four* or the omnipresence of money in *Keep the Aspidistra Flying*, unconquerable hegemony is a repeated feature of Orwell's fiction. Moreover, the second of Orwell's poems that was published in *The Adelphi*, 'A Dressed Man and a Naked Man' (1933) further outlines an engagement with such immovable social structures and suggests a thematic concern regarding hegemonic dominance that is indicative of his later novels. The structure of the poem suggests that within a dominant social model the actions of individuals and groups are ultimately irrelevant; an extension of this reading suggests that resistant activity which attempts to undermine, or indeed overthrow, hegemonic authority is similarly flawed. In other words, Orwell depicts certain power relationships that echo Gramscian notions of hegemony without offering counter-hegemonic potential.

The poem describes the comical haggling between a clothed man who is starving and a naked man with money as they negotiate a transaction of clothes from one man to the other (Orwell 2015: 31). The poem opens and ends with the lines 'A dressed man and a naked man / Stood by the kip-house fire', suggesting that the overarching social conditions remain static. In the course of the poem, the dressed man becomes naked and has the economic means for a meal and the naked man becomes fully clothed whilst now facing starvation. But the social relationship between the two men is unaltered, albeit reversed. Just as in this poem, both *Keep the Aspidistra Flying* and *Nineteen Eighty-Four* show social structures as static: Gordon Comstock and Winston Smith experience a dramatic reversal from insubordinates to conforming subjects whilst the relations of society remain the same as tactics of resistance are constrained within hegemonic authority. Orwell's exploration of inescapable social structures in this brief comedic poem provides the foundation for these novels and positions his poetry as an essential component to understanding his wider portrayal of hegemony and resistance. *Keep the Aspidistra Flying* and *The Adelphi* poems contain the seeds that developed and flowered into what is widely seen as the inherently political *Nineteen Eighty-Four*. Orwell's imagery of life and death in the narratives of rebellion and his depiction of performative conformity, which is termed by Scott as a 'mask', provides an imaginative space to reassess and extend theories of resistance (Scott 2002 [1985]: 93).

ORWELL'S LINGUISTIC PATTERNS OF RESISTANCE

The linguistic construction of resistance and dominance in Orwell's work reveals an interconnectedness between these opposing positions which undermines the insubordinate nature of rebellious rhetoric. James Scott's theorisation of a 'hidden transcript' suggests that dominated groups adopt actions and terminology of 'offstage speeches, gestures, and practices' to undermine the necessary conformity of that group, allowing the dominated a space of subtle insubordination (Scott 1990: 4). Yet the dominant group itself is described as having their own form of hidden transcript, representing 'the practices and claims of their rule that cannot be openly avowed' (ibid: xii). Orwell's portrayal of resistance sees the hidden transcripts of the dominant and dominated bodies merge into a single hidden transcript of hegemonic power. A Gramscian understanding of hegemony, where the dominated group adopts a 'conception which is not its own but is borrowed from another [hegemonic] group', is in this sense fused with Scott's notion of hidden transcripts to depict fundamentally flawed resistant activity (Gramsci 2002 [1971]: 62).

Winston's reading of 'the book' (*The Theory and Practice of Oligarchical Collectivism*), a text supposedly written by the Brotherhood to outline the overthrow of the Party, embodies this relationship between resistance and dominance by representing both the basis of revolutionary optimism and the unalterable authority of the Party. The transcript of the Brotherhood is described as telling Winston 'nothing that was new', his own thoughts are essentially contained within the text (Orwell 2013 [1949]: 229). But with Inner Party member O'Brien revealing that he himself collaborated in the production of 'the book', the Party is shown to contain, and be the origins of, the terms and logic of Winston's resistance. The hegemony of the Party extends to the principles of resistance that are expressed in 'the book' and manipulates the hidden transcript of the insubordinate in order to twist their logic into orthodoxy.

The novel further complicates notions of authority as terms of resistance are used by, and originate from, the Party. This is emphasised during Winston's and Julia's arrest by the Thought Police as the telescreen echoes Winston's claim that 'We are dead' by stating: 'You are dead' (ibid: 252). Here, the Party is shown to manipulate resistance through their observing apparatus which undermines notions of revolt whilst further reaffirming their overwhelming authority. The political significance of Winston accepting his death is thus claimed by, and becomes a product of, the Party. As Winston is drawn into a process of self-doubt and belittlement in the Ministry of Love, the realisation that O'Brien's mind '*contained* Winston's mind [original emphasis]' (ibid: 293) is reflective of the surveillance techniques available to the Party as they can monitor and adapt their approach to insubordinates, or subtly manipulate them, ensuring the hegemonic body can control transgressions against them. Thoughtcrime may still be possible, but the subversion of resistance into a reaffirmed dominance means that Winston and other rebels cannot escape the authority of the Party and their hidden transcripts necessarily remain within the influence of hegemony.

CONFORMITY AND LIFE

Winston's claim that 'We are dead' is echoed across Orwell's work through the linguistic construction of resistance as death. The notion that resistance and death have an intrinsic connection is suggested in the poem 'Sometimes in the Middle Autumn Days' (1933) where the persona reflects on their position amongst the 'death-marked people, they and I' (Orwell 2015: 28). By encouraging these people to 'remember / What tyrant holds your life in bond' an ambiguous social relationship of authority and subjection is constructed. The 'death-marked people' with whom the 'I' forms a community are associated with death by their very appearance whilst they are further described as 'men condemned'. The poem draws comparison with Scott's theorising of resistance through the connection made between active rebellion and death. The group hold back their rebellious consciousness until a moment of expression and certain death:

> Some thought, some faith, some meaning save,
>
> And speak it once before we go
>
> In silence to the silent grave.

The figure that holds their 'life in bond' is necessarily linked to the death of the group once they 'speak' their rebellious thoughts or act on their 'faith'. Much like Scott's suggestion that active rebellion will 'provoke a more rapid and ferocious response' than subtle resistance, the poem explores the repression of those who openly rebel (Scott 2002 [1985]: 93). The rebels are inescapably connected with death; conformity, by contrast, is described in relation to living. Not acting upon resistant thoughts and ideas is shown as a necessary component of survival. In the final stanza, the persona suggests that by holding back their open resistance, the group can continue their 'rout of life'. 'Rout' is significant here as it connotes a disorderly and disorganised group of people; life is only possible for the rebellious group when they remain as a secret and essentially inactive, unorganised group. Conformity is, thus, a requirement of survival and the poem suggests that the rebel must disown their unrest with the hegemonic tyrant or accept their death as a condition of resistance. The identity of the rebel is defined through death and, as the last stanza suggests, this fate is an inevitable consequence of an active rebellion.

Much like the 'death-marked people' in 'Sometimes in the Middle Autumn Days', Gordon's resistance in *Keep the Aspidistra Flying* is seen through the language of death, particularly when reflecting on his resistance against the hegemonic power of money in his claim that 'I am dead' (Orwell 2000 [1936]: 92). An understanding of resistance as death, and a subsequent rejection of life, is developed as it is the creation of life that prompts Gordon's eventual conformity. The realisation that Rosemary's pregnancy entails 'a bud of flesh, a bit of himself down there in her belly, alive and growing' (ibid: 253) forms a connection between the resistant Gordon and the living world of money; it is through creating a life that Gordon comes to accept his own.

The description of the rebel and society in terms of death is reversed as Gordon rejects the prospect of terminating the life of the foetus: 'Whatever happens we're not going to do *that*' (ibid). The living extension of himself inside of Rosemary prompts a realignment of the imagery and language of Gordon's resistance. His upcoming fatherhood sees his self-identification shift away from death towards living as he accepts the aspidistra, the symbol of middle-class conformity, as the 'tree of life' (ibid: 268) and acknowledges that he and Rosemary 'were *alive* [original emphasis]' (ibid). The role of money is not reimagined: Gordon is as shackled to money by the end of the novel as he is in the opening lines where 'money clinked in his trouser pocket' (ibid: 1) like chains of enslavement, but his attitude towards this dominance is shown to change. The resistant ideals of Gordon become values of acceptance as he embraces his role in creating life and living his own.

Gordon's understanding of life and death in relation to hegemony in *Keep the Aspidistra Flying* provides a conceptual basis for

Nineteen Eighty-Four. The inescapable influence of money and institutions of capitalism presents him with a choice between death through defeated resistance or the process of living as a subject of money. In *Nineteen Eighty-Four*, this dilemma is translated into the totalitarian setting of Airstrip One. Through the alteration of hegemonic authority from money to the Party, the connotations of life and death change; the Party has no need for consumers, and thus the choice of life that Gordon accepts is removed. Instead, life necessarily becomes death for the insubordinate as the acceptance of failed rebellion and love for Big Brother is unconsciously contained within the act of resistance. The moment of 'final, indispensable, healing change' (ibid: 342) comes for Winston as he imagines himself confessing to crimes and being executed: 'The long-hoped-for bullet was entering his brain' (ibid). Winston is, therefore, shown to hold death as representative of both his perceived rebellion and of subordination.

Winston never evades the control of the Party and his resistance is necessarily futile, which is reflected in his approach to death. His belief that those who rebel 'are the dead' (ibid: 156) is representative of his own position. He views resistance through the imagery of conformity as he can never truly rebel; the Brotherhood, 'the book', and O'Brien are all figures of the Party. Orwell's developing construction of resistance can be traced through his work as *Nineteen Eighty-Four* extends the portrayal of hegemonic authority in *Keep the Aspidistra Flying*, which in turn is embryonically explored through the relationship between death and resistance in 'Sometimes in the Middle Autumn Days'. The poem connects death and resistance and resonates with later Orwell works as the abstract hegemonic figure of the 'tyrant' is transferred into both a realist capitalist setting and an imagined totalitarian environment. Orwell in this way shows the death-centred hidden transcripts of dominated groups to be contained within overarching hegemonic narratives, as the language of resistance is necessarily contained within the logic of those who hold power.

MASKS AND RESISTANCE IN THE WRITING OF ORWELL

Scott's terminology can be of further use when considering the work of Orwell as the 'public mask of compliance' required of the subject is corrupted through Orwell's depiction of hegemonic power (Scott 2002 [1985]: 93). 'Sometimes in the Middle Autumn Days' is again informative, as the poem depicts a performative mask of conformity that is repeated in *Keep the Aspidistra Flying* and further complicated in *Nineteen Eighty-Four*. The persona is placed in subjection to hegemonic authority as they are shown as vulnerable in relation to the 'tyrant' who holds power over their life and the lives of the wider group. The assimilation of the persona into this group is emphasised as the term of identification in the poem shifts from 'I' to 'we' following the description of dominated people. The performative necessity of the group is described as the persona suggests they will 'live, hand, eye and brain, / Piously, outwardly, ever-aware'; the brain is shown to prompt a mask of an 'outwardly' conforming body that hides a rebellious consciousness that may challenge the dominant 'tyrant' figure.

Indeed, this forms the limit of tactical rebellion for the group. Although described as 'fighting, toiling as in a dream', the persona suggests that the only way in which the group can sustain any form of resistance is through an outward appearance of conformity. Scott's suggestion that a dominated group who face oppression must rebel in a way that 'never ventures to contest the formal definitions of hierarchy and power' has resonance with the poem as outward 'fighting' is replaced by the adoption of a mask (Scott 2002 [1985]: 93). The resistant thoughts of the group are separated from the actions of conformity as a necessary condition of responding to hegemony. Through the form of the novel, Orwell is able to extend the portrayal of tactical masks of conformity. For Gordon in *Keep the Aspidistra Flying* and Winston and Julia in *Nineteen Eighty-Four*, the identification of masks and, therefore, the indication of an insubordinate group, is shown as complex and problematic. The failure to decipher masks is further complicated as the hegemonic power itself is shown to adopt masks as a form of dominance. Orwell's poem thus provides an early conceptualisation of the tactics of resistance and ultimately dominance, which hold significance to the rebellions within his novels.

The adoption of masks in *Nineteen Eighty-Four* is a matter of survival, an opening description sees Winston 'set his features into the expression of quiet optimism which it was advisable to wear' (2013 [1949]: 7) while Gordon's mask is similarly shown as a necessity of employment and thus survival. Gordon's role when working in the bookshop is adaptive. He alters his mannerism and behaviour to suit the customer, ensuring he can interact as 'booklover to booklover' (2000 [1936]: 12), 'highbrow to highbrow' (ibid: 9) and 'lowbrow to lowbrow' (ibid: 18). The malleable necessity of the employee is further shown as his employment at the New Albion publishing agency requires him to adopt a persona that means he appears as 'just the same as any other City clerk' (ibid: 52) and that 'the people at the office never suspected him of unorthodox ideas' (ibid). Gordon is shown to understand the behaviour demanded of him by a market economy as he hides his resentment of this economic system through performing in the manner expected of him as an employee.

Gordon's failure to interpret the mask of others, however, emphasises the problematic nature of this form of resistance and foreshadows the difficulty Winston and Julia face in deciphering masks in *Nineteen Eighty-Four*. Scott's claims about masks suggests that groups of rebels can identify each other whilst shielding themselves from authority, yet masks are shown to be unnoticeable to Gordon. This is epitomised by his response to a barmaid at the Crichton Arms pub. Ben Clarke describes the barmaid as offering a performance: 'Her interactions with the customers are … a form of advertising' (Clarke 2015: 557). Despite his act of highbrow, lowbrow and City clerk, Gordon's self-awareness of masks fails to extend to an empathetic connection with a performing employee and he accepts the mask of the barmaid literally at face-value as he fantasises about 'a girl to flirt with' (2000 [1936]: 81) and is deceived by the very tactic that he himself adopts.

Although Winston and Julia share a desire to resist the Party, their initial responses to each other are entirely opposite. Whereas Julia can interpret Winston's public mask, he misunderstands the outward conformity of Julia as he is described as having 'disliked' Julia from the 'very first moment of seeing her' (2013 [1949]: 12), considering her as a member of the Thought Police, and debates murdering her when they pass outside of Charrington's shop. The immediate rebellious connection that Julia claims to have felt when first seeing Winston contrasts the 'black terror' he experiences at the 'sidelong glance' (ibid: 13) she gives him when passing in the Ministry of Truth. The 'everyday forms of resistance' that Scott sees as central to an insubordinate individual or community are thus misinterpreted as the disguise of Julia is shown to evade the perception of Winston (Scott 2002 [1985]: 95). It takes the bold, and observable, act of Julia passing a note to join the individual into something resembling a resistant group. Her actions show an awareness of public performance of conformity and she must break with her outward appearance whilst attempting to maintain an aura of subservience to connect with Winston. Ultimately, the public mask must be removed in order for it to be seen as this tactic provides an unstable basis for resistance.

HEGEMONIC MASKS AND THE SERVANT'S FACE

This problematic relationship between tactics of resistance and a necessary dominance is further complicated in *Nineteen Eighty-Four* by the face of O'Brien's servant, Martin. When meeting in O'Brien's flat to discuss their integration into the Brotherhood movement, O'Brien outlines the capability of the Brotherhood to 'alter people beyond recognition' (2013 [1949]: 200). Winston reflects that Martin has perhaps been subject to such alteration: as Martin looks as him blankly: 'It occurred to Winston that a synthetic face was perhaps incapable of changing its expression' (ibid: 201). Both the Party, through O'Brien, and the insubordinate Winston and Julia are portrayed as engaging in a project of deception. Winston's knowledge that a 'single flicker of the eye could give you away' (ibid: 42) encourages a separation between insubordinate thoughts and public representation of the self, whilst it is O'Brien's public appearance that lures Winston into a feeling of revolutionary potential. For Winston, Martin's 'synthetic' face represents the necessary emotionless coldness that is required between those in a group that opposes the hegemony of the Party; the face is a site of commitment to undermining the Party as it is fixed literally as a mask of 'synthetic' conformity.

However, as O'Brien's position within Party orthodoxy emerges, Winston's reflections are undermined as Martin's face embodies Party hegemony. Far from representing the Gramscian 'co-existence of two conceptions of the world' (Gramsci 2002 [1971]: 62) as a developmental stage of counter-hegemony, Martin's 'synthetic' appearance reflects the malleability of the individual under Party control and forms the Party ideal of being 'incapable of changing' (2013 [1949]: 201), thus ensuring permanent orthodoxy. The multiplicity of Martin highlights the intertwined tactics of resistance and domination in *Nineteen Eighty-Four*. Martin represents a figure who is balanced between the revolutionary bond that Winston imposes upon him as a member of the Brotherhood, and as a servant who shows conformity and submission to both his master and the Party. Although ultimately a figure of the Party, the face of Martin becomes a symbolic site of struggle between dominance and resistance which foreshadows the eventual failure of Winston's and Julia's resistance against the unquestionable dominance of the Party.

The tactics of resistance that Scott attributes to groups who experience domination are adopted by the Party and used against insubordinates; theories of resistance are, in this way, reimagined in *Nineteen Eighty-Four* as tactics of dominance. O'Brien hides his conformity and role within the structures of the Party through a veil of apparent unorthodoxy by holding an appearance that suggests to Winston when their eyes meet that 'an unmistakable message' (2013 [1949]: 21) of shared contempt towards the Party has passed between them. Resistance is not covert as the Party itself echoes the tactics of resistance in their own monitoring techniques. O'Brien both embodies the ideas of resistance in which Winston and Julia are engaged and also highlights the futility of such tactics. Resistance is shown to be contained within the Party and the 'public mask of compliance' is subverted by the hegemonic group as their dominance engulfs and manipulates those who attempt to resist.

Tactics of resistance are destabilised as Julia's faith in 'judging people by their faces' (2013 [1949]: 175) becomes the means by which the Party ensnare Winston. Daphne Patai suggests this inversion of tactics of resistance is a logical extension to hegemony as she claims the Party 'depends on a supply of opponents' (Patai 1984: 223). Patai argues that the position of power embodied by O'Brien is dependent on a game-like relationship with a resistant figure and the novel follows Winston's moulding into, and fulfilment of, that role. This claim challenges the notion of complete hegemony as a target of authority, instead showing that total control would eliminate the rebellious figures that the hegemonic body requires. Patai interprets the Party as engaging in 'theatrical play' which entices the focus of their game, Winston, into their trap (ibid: 226). Resistance, and tactics of resistance, are not only placed within Party dominance, but are a construct of the Party. This sees the Gramscian notion of hegemony and Scott's 'hidden transcript' of resistance combine to produce a dominant power that wishes to encourage a sense of its own vulnerability in order to promote the resistance that its power depends upon. Perfect hegemony for the Party is imperfect control, allowing for people like Winston to resist and be crushed over and over again.

THE PERMANENT MASK OF THE DEFEATED REBEL

The re-entering of the defeated rebel into the world of hegemonic dominance, however, marks a significant shift in the role of masks. In the closing chapter of *Keep the Aspidistra Flying*, Gordon is shown to embrace the expectations of the money-world, taking pleasure in the instalment-purchased furniture in his newly rented home with Rosemary, whilst insisting that an aspidistra is 'the proper thing to have' (2000 [1936]: 276). Gordon ends the novel as an extension of his bookshop persona as highbrow and lowbrow. His performative role is transformed into his self; the mask becomes a permanent fixture as the rebel accepts his place in subjection to hegemonic structures. Terry Eagleton emphasises this as he argues that Gordon's views are a reflection of the bourgeois class: Gordon is, therefore, 'bound to the world he rejects by a simple inversion' (Eagleton 1974: 25). Gordon's resistance follows the logic of the very authority he seeks to resist and in this way his mask always holds the potential to become his self as resistance is a contradiction of his own logic. The rebellious logic of Gordon is constructed, as Lynette Hunter notes, through the 'types' and 'clichés' on which bourgeois society itself is based; he connects his unattractiveness to women with his lack of money and seeks to reduce his personal failings to the simple diagnosis of finance (Hunter 1984: 178-179). His rebellious values are necessarily contained within the hegemonic structures of authority and his ability to produce advertising copy emphasises this: he merely needs to invert his logic of resistance to become a flourishing figure in the money-world. Performance and reality merge as Gordon's mask is understood as effectively representing himself. The authority and power of money that he resists for so long eventually prompts a subtle shift in his thinking which transforms him from a starving poet into a lower-middle-class ideal.

The defeat of Winston and Julia results in striking physical changes that represent their masks becoming their permanent selves:

Winston's facial features are described as having 'thickened' (2013 [1949]: 332) whilst Julia's waist 'had grown thicker' (ibid: 335). The features that previously indicated resistance through a mask of conformity – Winston's face, which Julia read as knowing 'you were against *them*' (ibid: 140) and Julia's waist, which had a 'sash, with the emblem of the Junior Anti-Sex League' (ibid: 12), whilst also signifying her sexual rebellion – have thickened as underlying conformity is crushed and the mask becomes the self. Much like Gordon, the mask of conformity they previously wore as a temporary tactic of resistance has 'thickened' into permanence. Whereas Gordon's mask takes an ideological form as it is his actions and words that show resistance, in *Nineteen Eighty-Four* this resistance is expressed in a more physical way. The mental and physical torture and degradation of Winston and Julia crushes their rebellion, yet has further importance in providing the basis for bodily healing. This recovery, alongside the mentally altered state of the rebel, allows for the body to represent their change and conformity. The emphasis given to the thickening of Julia's waist and Winston's face shows tactics of resistance becoming the basis for a literal embodiment of conformity and the victory of the Party in the hegemonic game.

JULIA: THE HEGEMONIC MASK?

Julia's role in the novel is the subject of much critical speculation. Gordon Bowker's suggestion that Julia herself may be a product of the state apparatus, and that she plays a central role in luring Winston 'straight into the arms of the Thought Police', would necessitate a complete re-evaluation of her rebellion as she would instead emerge as the most powerful and effective Party figure in the novel (2003: 388-389). The physical changes she is shown to have undergone in her final meeting with Winston could be a result of bodily alterations similar to those seen through the servant Martin, rather than from torture, or as a means of further monitoring Winston through the mask of a defeated rebel. In this sense, Winston's initial interpretation of Julia as a figure of the Party to fear would have been correct. Ironically, this would be the only instance in which Winston correctly judges a mask related to Party hegemony. The approach taken in this paper towards the adoption and interpretation of masks positions Julia as a genuine rebel as Winston's characteristic failure in deciphering masks creates a flawed logic of resistance that views her as an enemy whilst believing O'Brien, Charrington and Martin to be sympathisers in his struggle against the Party.

Masks, then, are a significant feature of Orwell's depiction of resistance as they evolve from Scott's static model of resistance in 'Sometimes in the Middle Autumn Days' into what becomes a symbol of authority and domination in *Keep the Aspidistra Flying* and *Nineteen Eighty-Four*. Masks are transformed from providing a space of defiance into a reaffirmation of the permeating qualities of hegemony. The experience of Gordon, alongside Winston and Julia, suggests that masks themselves bind the rebel to authority and undermine resistance. The development of this form of insubordination consequently challenges Scott's description of the 'mask of public compliance' as Orwell's conception of such performativity connects the mask with the conforming self of the defeated rebel (Scott 2002 [1985]: 93).

CONCLUSIONS

An understanding of theoretical accounts of resistance can be complicated through a consideration of George Orwell's writings. Gramsci's work on hegemony provides a theoretical touchstone for Orwell's depiction of unalterable dominance as resistance to hegemonic social relations is subverted into a reaffirmation of authority and power. This, in turn, complicates Scott's accounts of resistance by groups who cannot overthrow their oppressors as Orwell presents literary settings in which hegemony gives no space for such activity; it is in this way that an insubordinate 'mask of public compliance' can be reimagined as a tactic of hegemonic dominance (ibid: 93). Resistance is a predominant theme in Orwell's writings, yet it is ironic that the term can ultimately be reconsidered to imply and incorporate dominance. His poetic contributions to *The Adelphi* lay the foundations of his construction, and undermining, of resistance in his later novels as the permanent hegemonic authorities in *Keep the Aspidistra Flying* and *Nineteen Eighty-Four* develop the language and tactics of resistant activity first enacted in his poems. Although these ideas are in many ways typified in Orwell's final novel, drawing on the origins of such ideas in his earlier work enables a sustained and progressive understanding of Orwell and resistance. The hegemonic settings of these texts condemn the process of resistance as a predetermined failure. Power and responsibility are portrayed in a manner that surpasses the work of Scott and Gramsci as the imaginative potential of Orwell's writing provides a new basis for theoretical engagement with resistance.

REFERENCES

Bowker, Gordon (2003) *George Orwell*, New York: Little, Brown

Clarke, Ben (2015) 'Beer and cigarettes and a girl to flirt with': Orwell, drinking and the everyday, *English Studies*, Vol. 96, No. 5 pp 541-561

Eagleton, Terry (1974) Orwell and the lower-middle-class novel, Williams, Raymond (ed.) *George Orwell: A Collection of Critical Essays*, New Jersey: Spectrum pp 10-33

Gramsci, Antonio (1971) *Selections from the Prison Notebooks*, Hoare, Quintin and Nowell Smith, Geoffrey (eds and trans) New York: International Publishers pp 323-334 in Duncombe, Stephen (ed.) *Cultural Resistance Reader* (2002) London: Verso pp 58-67

Hoffman, John (1984) *The Gramscian Challenge*, Oxford: Basil Blackwell

Hunter, Lynette (1984) Stories and voices in Orwell's early narratives, Norris,

Christopher (ed.) *Inside the Myth: Orwell: Views From the Left*, London: Lawrence and Wishart pp 163-182

Orwell, George (2000) *George Orwell: Essays*, London: Penguin

Orwell, George (2000 [1936]) *Keep the Aspidistra Flying*, London: Penguin

Orwell, George (2013 [1949]) *Nineteen Eighty-Four*, London: Penguin

Orwell, George (2015) *George Orwell: The Complete Poetry*, Venables, Dione (ed.) London: Finlay Publisher

Orwell, George (1970) *The Collected Essays, Journalism and Letters of George Orwell*, Orwell, Sonia and Angus, Ian (eds) Vol. 4, Middlesex: Penguin

Orwell, George (1998) *The Complete Works of George Orwell*, Davison, Peter (ed.) Vol. 17, London: Secker & Warburg

Patai, Daphne (1984) *The Orwell Mystique: A Study in Male Ideology*, Massachusetts: The University of Massachusetts Press

Rodden, John and Rossi, John (2012) *The Cambridge Introduction to George Orwell*, Cambridge: Cambridge University Press

Scott, James (1990) *Domination and the Arts of Resistance: Hidden Transcripts*, New Haven: Yale University Press

Scott, James (1985) *Weapons of the Weak: Everyday Forms of Peasant Resistance*, New Haven: Yale University Press pp 29-36, in *Cultural Resistance Reader* (2002) Duncombe, Stephen (ed.) London: Verso pp 89-96

NOTE ON THE CONTRIBUTOR

Harry Bark is a postgraduate student at the University of Oxford studying towards an MSt in English (1830-1914). He completed his undergraduate studies at the University of Leeds and wrote his dissertation on George Orwell and theories of resistance.

REVIEWS

Churchill & Orwell: The Fight for Freedom
Thomas E. Ricks
Penguin Press, New York, 2017 pp 340
ISBN 978 1 59420 6139

This is a lively and well-written book that is meant for the general reader. There is a great popularity at the moment among publishers and presumably the reading public for short books on familiar topics. Included in that current interest are short biographies of well-known figures. Apparently quite a few like to read further studies of those who have already had one or more biographies rather than first biographies of lesser known men and women. It is true that it is perfectly legitimate to reconsider well-known figures, to re-assess them in terms of our present pre-occupations or on the basis of new information that has become available. That is certainly a valid way to go forward as such discussions can frequently yield new insights and provide illumination on our present concerns and discontents and on the individuals themselves. Certain figures remain subject to continual interest. That has certainly been true not only for Churchill but for Orwell as well despite predictions in the 1960s that interest in Orwell would fade. The recent establishment of this very journal is evidence of that. As Ricks points out, the rise of the surveillance state and the growing and, indeed, the somewhat terrifying capacities of the computer have made Orwell's *Nineteen Eighty-Four* increasingly relevant. In a sense the novel is a warning of how a socialist state, because of the leaders' lust for power, can become a tyranny of the worst sort. This text was completed before the Trump administration did so much for sales of the book through the terms 'alternative facts' and 'fake news'.

One might have expected that this study would be an imaginative interplay between Churchill and Orwell. Rather it is almost exclusively an interesting but not particularly original set of alternative chapters telling the life story of the two men. Not surprisingly, they did not know one another as they hardly moved in the same worlds. Churchill did read *Nineteen Eighty-Four* twice. Ricks does not, as he could have, make anything of the point that Orwell first used the phrase 'the Cold War' and that Churchill did so much to increase awareness of its existence through his famous coining of the 'Iron Curtain'. The juxtaposition of the two men as fighters for freedom is valid. But they did so in such different ways, Churchill as the most important leader in keeping the battle going against Hitler when Europe was conquered and Russia and the United States had not yet entered the war. Orwell fought for freedom in a radically different fashion, emphasising the importance of freedom of speech, resisting a regime's wish to exercise thought control and to have the ability to rewrite the past to conform to the current party line.

For the readers of this journal, Ricks' account will hardly tell them anything new. If anything, they may disagree, as I do, with Ricks' very low assessment of Orwell's 1930s novels. And Orwell, though far from famous, was a somewhat better known figure in the literary world of the 1930s than Ricks allows.

Ricks hardly explores the most intriguing juxtaposition between the two men. The central figure of *Nineteen Eighty-Four* is Winston Smith which to any reader conjures up as a name some suggestion of Winston Churchill. And he mentions that Simon Schama, in his television series, *A History of Britain* (2000), entitles its final section 'The Two Winstons'. The biographies of the two men make up virtually the total content of the episode. In many ways Schama is very similar to this book; he uses the contrasting stories of two such different men to tell the history of Britain up to the conclusion of the Second World War. Yet Schama is more vivid and effective than Ricks. He agrees with Ricks that what was most important about the two men, although their values and lives were so different, was their commitment to freedom. More than Ricks, as a historian he puts more emphasis on the importance of knowing the past as a way of preserving the values and liberties of the present and future. But Schama, too, does not speculate on the reasons why Orwell named his central figure in *Nineteen Eighty-Four* Winston Smith.

The two Winstons were both fighting for what they believed in. Churchill won, Smith lost. Nevertheless his rebellion against the regime in his affair with Julia, his hatred of Big Brother, his attempt to maintain that two plus two equal four, despite his ultimate defeat, makes him someone who at least attempted to resist. But he is an everyman figure which could hardly be said of Churchill. Orwell admired Churchill's wartime leadership but he was certainly aware that Churchill was not the person to shape the needed transformation of British society. In *The Lion and the Unicorn* (1941), he argued that radical changes were necessary if Britain were to win the war. He later realised that, sadly, that transformation was not to happen. He was a strong supporter of the welfare state which Churchill was not. However much Orwell may be coopted by the right, he was after Spain committed to socialism, as he conceived of it. Orwell commented from time to time about Churchill in his writings but he was not a major interest of his.

REVIEW

Ricks highlights the fact that Orwell's last publication was a review of Churchill's *Their Finest Hour*, the second volume of his Second World War memoirs. The left-wing American journal, *The New Leader*, had written to him asking him to write some reviews for it. Orwell agreed and asked the journal to suggest a book that he might write about. In reply, the journal suggested the Churchill book or an edition of letters by Marcel Proust. Orwell not surprisingly chose Churchill. In concluding the review, he wrote: 'Whether or not 1940 was anyone else's finest hour, it was certainly Churchill's. However much one may disagree with him, however thankful one may be that he and his party did not win the 1945 election, one has to admire in him not only his courage but also a certain largeness and geniality which comes out even in formal memoirs of this type, much less personal than a book like *My Early Life*' (*CWGO*, Vol. 20: 113). This was published on 14 May 1949 but it was not actually his last publication. That appeared the next day in *The New York Times* books section, a review of Hesketh Pearson's biography of Dickens, a subject much closer to Orwell's heart.

So why did Orwell use Winston as the first name of his central character? My hunch is that it was because Orwell was to a degree admiring of Churchill and to a degree being ironic about him. Winston Smith in a non-Churchillian way was trying to be heroic. But he was much more a lower middle-class everyman rather than a political leader from the upper classes. *Churchill & Orwell* is valuable in reminding us through its brief biographies of the great contributions of these two men whom one might not ordinarily consider together. It is a good read but it doesn't provide much in terms of new insights or information about either.

Peter Stansky,
Stanford University

George Orwell and Religion
Michael G. Brennan
Bloomsbury Academic, London, 2017 pp 184
ISBN 978 1 4725 3073 8

Why write a book about George Orwell and religion? It isn't that there is no religion in Orwell, but of all the important things that mattered to Orwell and his work – including ideology, class, empire, gender, language, history and truth – most people would not place religion high on the list. Orwell was not a religious man. He lost his religious faith early and permanently and without regret. It's true that his second novel was about a clergyman's daughter, that he knew the Bible well, that he asked to be buried according to the rites of the Church of England and that he opined that there was hardly a town in the south of England where you could throw a brick without hitting the niece of a bishop.

These incidental facts are not what Michael Brennan is after. It is his argument that it is no exaggeration to say that 'Orwell simply could not leave religion alone, not only in his private correspondence and notebooks but also in his published fiction, journalism and reviews' (p. xi). Later in his preface he makes a wider claim: 'Orwell's pronouncements on the place of religion in society remain of paramount importance to a meaningful understanding of his writings and their continued relevance for a modern-day readership' (p. xix). Paramount importance? If Brennan can convince us that religion was central to Orwell's view of the world and that his ideas about religion are essential to an understanding of his work, some of us are going to have to think again about this writer.

REVIEW

Brennan has gone to work with vigour. It sometimes seems as if he may have gone through and underlined all the religious references and phraseology in the *Complete Works*. There is plenty to gather. Since Orwell and almost everyone else in the England of his day had had a Christian upbringing, such phraseology is written into their everyday language. His tramps know the Bible stories and remember the words of hymns. What exactly does this prove? The hostel in 'The Spike' (of 1931) is described as a 'purgatory': is this religious writing? Sometimes the search goes further afield. Conrad Noel, later notorious as the 'Red Vicar' of Thaxted, was once curate in the parish in Paddington where Orwell's aunt Ida lived. Brennan feels that Noel and Orwell had much in common as upper-middle-class socialists and that it is 'likely' Noel's anti-Catholic views played a formative role in developing Orwell's own antipathy towards the Church of Rome (pp 5-6). Perhaps. But Noel is nowhere mentioned in Orwell's writing.

This book identifies anti-Catholicism and anti-semitism as two lifelong themes of Orwell's discussions of religion. A casual prejudice against papists and Jews was a quite common piece of kit in the inherited culture of English people brought up in Orwell's class and time. But if you place end-to-end all of Orwell's hostile remarks about the Church of Rome throughout his career, as Brennan does, the prejudice does start to look like an obsession, impervious to history and circumstance. The Catholic population of Britain almost doubled in Orwell's lifetime, but how much did he actually know about its members? Throughout his writing career he nourished what Brennan nicely calls 'an incorruptible pessimism' over the motives and actions of the Church (p. 157). Can this go back to his early schooling (from 1908-1911) with the Ursuline nuns at Henley?

Brennan is both puzzled and angered by the often crude anti-Catholicism to be found, for example, in *The Road to Wigan Pier*, an instance of Orwell's tendency towards 'hectoring and factually hazy polemic in which documentary truth and factual accuracy become distinctly secondary to the angry, sneering rhetorical impact of his denunciations' (pp 57-58). The notebooks show that he did actually gather detailed information about religious matters, and the social and charitable work of the churches, in his research in the north, but he excluded almost all of it from the published book. Brennan is shocked at Orwell's indifference to verifying his facts about Catholicism and other established religions, claiming this as evidence of his subject's 'ingrained religious bigotry' (p. 73).

This is fascinating stuff. In one chapter after another, *George Orwell and Religion* puzzles over this hostility, though in the end perhaps we need go no further than the writer's sense of the Church of Rome's more formidable organisation and reach, and desire for power and influence in public affairs, than that of its Protestant rivals. Most of its adherents could be relied on to take a reactionary stance on issues of the day, and its dogma and hierarchy of authority looked to Orwell like a potentially totalitarian structure. His strongest antipathy seems to have been against Catholic intellectuals, and among them against converts. In 'Notes on Nationalism', an important essay of 1945, he listed 'political Catholicism' among examples of pernicious 'nationalism' – 'the habit of identifying oneself with a single nation or other unit, placing it beyond good and evil and recognising no other duty than that of advancing its interests'. It is hard to imagine the 'poor, unoffending old Church of England' (p. 32) qualifying to join that list. And, to make an obvious point, he had some affection for the Church of England because it was English. Besides being relatively harmless, it was part of a familiar cherished world.

As for anti-semitism, there are plenty of instances of it in Orwell, especially, as Brennan notes, in *Down and Out*, in this respect 'a problematic and distasteful text' (p. 36). This is not to be excused although, like others such as T. S. Eliot, he corrected that 'stupid, suburban prejudice' (as Ezra Pound was to call it) when he became aware of the Nazi persecution of Jews in the thirties. He writes about the Jews as an ethnic group, but never shows much curiosity about Judaism, and his essay 'Anti-Semitism in Britain' (1945), well discussed here (pp 109-111), has very little to say about religion. Prejudice against Jews was a significant social phenomenon, rather than a matter of religious difference. The persecution of the Jews, under Hitler and Stalin, was perhaps the vilest crime of the ideological dictatorships that Orwell set his face against. The full details of the Holocaust emerging after the defeat of Germany and the Nuremberg trials of 1945-1946 were fresh and raw when *Nineteen Eighty-Four* was being written. Winston Smith is not a Jew. But it would have been hard to write (or read) about a victim of totalitarian cruelty in those years and *not* think about the fate of the Jews of Europe and Russia, and that memory does, indeed, haunt Orwell's last novel.

Yet it is strange that a writer so often hostile to religion should have been, apparently, so uninterested in religious belief. Even in *A Clergyman's Daughter* (1935), he is a lot more concerned with what the Church does, and stands for, than with why and what religious faith means to the individual. He mistrusted religious institutions but was fairly unconcerned, and perhaps ignorant, about individual faith. Not himself feeling a need for faith, it may have been a subject that bored him. Unlike his contemporaries Graham Greene and Evelyn Waugh (both subjects of books by Michael Brennan), Orwell seems to have had no interest in theology.

REVIEW

Orwell had spent five years in Burma and learned several Oriental languages. What about his attitudes to Buddhism or Hinduism? E. M. Forster knew a lot less about the East than Orwell. But the careful attention given to religion in *A Passage to India* (1924) contrasts with its relatively perfunctory presence in Orwell's Burmese writing. The portrayal of U Po Kyin's Buddhism in *Burmese Days* is strictly cartoonish. To the narrator of 'A Hanging' (1931), the Hindu calling on his god on the scaffold is making an inexplicable and embarrassing noise.

Many people in the twentieth century, at least in Europe, felt that the age of religious faith was coming to an end. Orwell was of their number, though he retained some nostalgic affection for the remains of Christianity – like the sight of old maids biking to Holy Communion through the mists of the autumn mornings, conjured in *The Lion and the Unicorn* (1941). He felt that religious belief was withering away in ordinary people. In his own time, the totalitarian ideologies of Hitler and Stalin, with what Orwell called their 'power-worship', had made a bid to fill the vacuum of faith.

But he still looked forward to, and fought for, a future of intellectual freedom for all in a secular society. Without a belief in the afterlife, people would need to work out a system of good and evil that did not depend on divine sanction. Those who had been brought up as Christians often felt that it made sense to embrace the baby of Christian morality after throwing out the bathwater of Christian eschatology and the Church. Orwell was certainly a moralist, and his morality was largely consistent with Christian moral teaching. He had some admiration for Christian socialists like Jacques Maritain but in the end, as Brennan admits, he 'saw no way of reconciling the other-worldliness of Christianity with worldly Socialism' (p. 122). His suspicion of other-worldliness extended to the sainted Gandhi, whose asceticism, Orwell thought, seemed grounded in a dislike of ordinary human bodily life. He may have been sometimes unfair to religion, and especially to Catholicism. But his attitude to it, like his attitude to the bullying ideologies he thought it resembled, was consistently humanist and democratic.

Brennan writes of 'Orwell's anxieties over the loss of a sense of the religious in modern society' (p. 136). But I feel this is not quite the right way to put it. Established religion was in decline, at least in Europe, and the totalitarian ideologies that had rushed in to fill the opening void had to be resisted and overcome. Then there was the danger that in a materialistic machine age of high capitalism, there would be nothing for people to believe in. This perception, however, did not really amount to an Orwellian anxiety over the loss of a sense of the religious. There was plenty for people to believe in and work for – democracy, truth, fairness – and these things could be framed in entirely secular ways. A writer could help in articulating, debating, refining, defending and, to an extent, implementing these values.

The destination of Brennan's argument – as in the teleology of most Orwell criticism – is *Nineteen Eighty-Four* (1949). He has an excellent discussion of the presence of religious motifs and ideas (the worship of Big Brother, O'Brien as confessor, and so on), and the linkage of religious and political totalitarianism in the novel. But he wants to go further, writing of 'Orwell's preoccupation in *Nineteen Eighty-Four* with society's loss of inner spirituality and external religious frameworks' (p. 141). Placing the book in 'a vigorous English tradition of politicized religious writing', he claims that 'the novel offers a sombre religious meditation on the fallen state of humankind' (p. 146). I don't really recognise *Nineteen Eighty-Four* in these descriptions. If 'the fallen state of humankind' means anything stronger than simple human weakness, it has to be in the context of a Christian soteriological narrative. Is this present in *Nineteen Eighty-Four*, or anywhere else in Orwell? Is there any sense in Orwell of a transcendent spiritual existence, the possibility of spiritual salvation and an afterlife? Isn't the Orwell of the last published novel still the most worldly, the most anti-transcendental and, of course, the most anti-utopian of writers?

Of the two claims mentioned at the start of this review, Michael Brennan has gone a fair way to proving the first, that in his writing Orwell simply could not leave religion alone. He has made the best case that could be made for the second claim, about the paramount importance of his views about religion in society for our understanding of Orwell and his contemporary relevance. If in the end this argument doesn't convince, it has produced a book in which anybody interested in Orwell will find much that is fascinating and insightful.

Orwell was wrong, or at least short-sighted for once, in his belief that religious faith was dying out in the world. Now that we live in a new century where faith has proved to be as vital (and mortal) an issue as in the middle ages, you can see why Michael Brennan feels that Orwell's writing about the subject might be an important part of his continued relevance for a modern-day readership. What on earth would George Orwell find to say about the painful struggles that express themselves today as conflicts between, and within, religious groups and between believers and non-believers? We can say confidently that he was against fundamentalism of all kinds. But did he understand, any better than the rest of us, how to deal with it?

Douglas Kerr,
University of Hong Kong

REVIEW

We Know All About You: The Story of Surveillance in Britain and America

Rhodri Jeffreys-Jones

Oxford University Press, Oxford, 2017 pp 290

ISBN 978 0 19 874966 0

Orwell's *Nineteen Eighty-Four*, though first published in 1949, still stands as probably the most influential depiction of a Big Brother society in which state-controlled surveillance intrudes into the most intimate aspects of citizens' lives. As Peter Marks comments (2015: 14): 'The disembodied emblem of the Party (never seen in the flesh and only ever viewed in posters 'plastered everywhere'), Big Brother remains a potent symbol of totalitarian power and of invasive monitoring.'

In this outstanding, brief overview of the history of surveillance and debates surrounding it in the UK and US, University of Edinburgh academic Rhodri Jeffreys-Jones challenges head-on Orwell's representation of the secret state in his celebrated dystopian novel. According to Jeffreys-Jones, Orwell concentrated exclusively on state surveillance thus ignoring the crucial role of private snooping. Moreover, spying on working people has been the dominant feature in the history of surveillance – yet too often ignored by historians.

For Jeffreys-Jones, the rise of Europe's nation states, the growth of military organisation, urbanisation and of capitalism all contributed to the development of surveillance. He continues (p. 12-13): 'The United States, however, took the lead. Contrary to the assumptions of those who have concentrated on the role of the organized state, it was the distinctively American combination of weak government and strong business that underpinned the rise of surveillance.' An early example of private surveillance occurred on the slave plantations of rural America. But the world's first major surveillance operation resulted from the development of the credit rating industry. Agents 'made local inquiries into merchants' credit-worthiness, often equating it with moral characteristics. Under instruction from their boss, they would look for signs of sexual licence, slothfulness and drunkenness as well, of course, dishonesty. In building the profiles of potential clients, they paid heed to factors like ethnicity, age and business history. The credit reporters also checked tax assessments, lawsuits, bankruptcy proceedings and financial statements' (p. 15).

While in the 19th century, no government activity remotely approached the scale of credit surveillance, however, at federal level there were developments: in 1790, Congress supplied President George Washington a 'contingency fund' to pay for spies – and the privilege of not having to account for how he spent it. Later, the Office of Naval Intelligence (formed in 1882) and the Military Information Division (1885) would not engage in domestic surveillance until the twentieth century. In the UK, numerous police spies operated in an attempt to frustrate the franchise movement (p. 19). Then in 1873 the Intelligence Branch of the War Office was formed – while a decade later the Irish Special Branch was created within Scotland Yard to combat the rise of violent Irish nationalism and the Naval Intelligence Department came into being.

By the early twentieth century, private detectives (immortalised in Arthur Conan-Doyles's Sherlock Holmes) in both the UK and US constituted a substantial industry (p. 20). In the UK, Admiral Reginald 'Blinker' Hall set up the Economic League in 1926, providing blacklists of radical trade unionists to employers (p. 27). Meanwhile, in the States, corporate surveillance of workers intensified. Col. Ralph Van Deman compiled lists of trade union activists nationwide. 'When he circulated his data to potential employers, they served as a blacklist. If you were on that blacklist, you did not get a job' (p. 26). Jeffreys-Jones argues (p. 28): 'Aimed as it was against working people and not the articulate middle classes [and I guess we can include Orwell in this group], blacklisting has not figured in the traditional litany of surveillance excesses.'

By the 1930s, the Pinkerton National Detective Agency, founded in 1850, was conducting massive snooping on workers – as revealed during hearings of the La Follete Civil Liberties Committee of the

Senate (p. 72). General Motors could not conceal the fact that it had spent around $1 million on informers within the United Automobile Workers Union (ibid). At the state level, close watch was held on radical intellectuals. By the end of the 1930s there were FBI files on Clifford Odets, Ernest Hemingway, John Steinbeck, Pearl Buck, William Faulkner and Upton Sinclair, the Atlantic solo flyer Charles Lindbergh and the historian Harry Elmer Barnes (pp 82-89).

Even as Orwell was penning his dystopian masterpiece on his Scottish island refuge, 'Vansittartism' was creeping into the core of British life. Named after its architect, the senior diplomat, Sir Robert, later Lord Vansittart, Jeffreys-Jones describes it as a silent (and, therefore, more insidious) form of McCarthyism – involving the blacklisting of BBC employees and the hounding of Church of England vicars (p. 30).

By the 21st century, private enterprises continued to play crucial roles in the security state. In the US for instance, the Office of the Director of National Intelligence reported in 2007 that more than 37,000 private contractors worked for the federal government on covert operations and security matters (p, 33). In the UK, a focus here is on the Hackgate controversy (highlighted in the Leveson Inquiry in 2011) – and the snooping conducted by the corporate press (pp 185-186). Later chapters take in a wide variety of subjects including the surveillance of Communist Party and Socialist Workers Party members, black civil rights campaigners, feminists and pacifists in the US, Special Branch snooping on Jeremy Corbyn (later to be leader of the Labour Party), evidence that almost 75 per cent of American companies monitored worker communication – and the intensification of the activities of the secret state post 9/11 in both the US and UK (pp 187-219).

REVIEW

Jeffreys-Jones concludes that, in terms of harm done to people on a daily basis, private surveillance (ignored by Orwell) outperforms its public counterpart (p. 243). Yet, a consistent anti-statist preoccupation runs through Orwell, the Church investigations into US intelligence in the wake of Watergate during the mid-1970s and the revelations of highly intrusive global surveillance by US/UK intelligence agencies by the former NSA contractor, Edward Snowden in 2013.

Some of Jeffreys-Jones's other conclusions are distinctly off-target. For instance, he says (p. 244): 'The surveillance branches of the US and UK intelligence communities have in recent years behaved relatively well, to the best of our knowledge.' Moreover, the book is lacking a theoretical edge that could highlight the private sector not as autonomous from the state in advanced capitalist societies but economically, politically and ideologically closely tied to it.

But overall, the author has presented a convincing critique of Orwellian statism – directing our attention to the (too often marginalised) role of private surveillance in the security state.

REFERENCE

Marks, Peter (2015) George Orwell and the history of surveillance studies, Keeble, Richard Lance (ed.) *George Orwell Now!*, Bury St Edmunds: Abramis pp 13-29

Richard Lance Keeble,
University of Lincoln and Liverpool Hope University

Incognito Social Investigation in British Literature: Certainties in Degradation

Luke Seaber

Palgrave Macmillan, Cham, 2017 pp 274

ISBN 978 3 31 950961 7

This is a fascinating study that explores the genre of writings produced by 'incognito social investigators' from the 1860s to more recent times. The author identifies James Greenwood as the inventor of the genre, and locates his approach against other writers such as J.H. Stallard, Olive Christian Malvery, George Orwell and Polly Toynbee, as well as less well known works by Robin Page and Stephen Reynolds. This review needs to be predicated by the caveat that I have read and reviewed this as a historian and not as a literary studies expert. That said, many of these texts scrutinised are ones that I use for both research and teaching purposes because of my particular interests in the history of homelessness in modern Britain. And the question historians have always been confronted with is to what extent are these apparent explorations of the underbelly of society either fictionalised or highly selective in their exposés.

Over eight chapters the analysis moves from exploring the development of the genre from James Greenwood's 1866 account of a night in the workhouse to its highpoint with Orwell – but crucially also attempting to locate a series of post-1945 studies into this genre. An analysis is made of the narratives of tramping, before evaluation of those investigators who disguised themselves to work amongst the poor and consideration of those who chose to live amongst their investigative subjects. Importantly, the role that female investigators played throughout the nineteenth and twentieth centuries is given the centrality it deserves.

Although he admits his primary concern is with the text form and theoretical questions of construction, Seaber does find himself drawn, in his often forensic analysis, towards the validity of the historical detail, and in doing so the analysis provides convincing explanations for how, and why, readers ought to be less sceptical of their value as historical text. The undoubted hero of this entire study is Orwell and especially his *Down and Out in Paris and London* 'the masterpiece of the form' (p. 73) – but more of this below.

It is necessary to explain why Seaber has settled on the term 'incognito social investigator'. Although admitting the term is unwieldy, Seaber feels the action of using disguise to enable social investigation with a concern for social change makes this preferable to other terms such as 'slummers' or 'down and outers' or 'class passers'.

The methodological conceptual tool employed in order to evaluate the method of writing and production used by the authors under scrutiny is drawn from anthropology. It is the idea of 'etic' and 'emic'. The author is being 'etic' when they are describing or evaluating something according to their (or their group's) criteria, whereas they are being 'emic' when they are describing or reviewing matters in relation to the subject's, or the subject's group's, criteria.

At face value, Orwell's *Down and Out* does not fit within the Greenwoodian genre. It is highly fictionalised. It does not present itself as an incognito study. Seaber's point is that Orwell wants to be seen as someone plunged unprepared into poverty, thus enabling him to assert his expertise on the subject as one who has truly known poverty. Seaber considers Orwell as muddling the etic and emic approaches in which he attempts to disguise his expertise and public school background in order to ensure he is deeper undercover and absorbed into the underworld than previous social investigators. Ultimately, Seaber sees Orwell's work as a 'boundary stone marking the genre's end' (p 73). Writers of the post-1945 generation knew they could not surpass Orwell. Furthermore, the world of the tramps was rapidly changing in the years after the 1948 National Assistance Act as the casual wards were replaced with a depleted network of Reception Centres and the Common Lodging Houses network declined.

For the historian there is much unpick, and reflect upon, within this volume. The challenge to Seth Koven's reading of Greenwood's inability to effectively disguise himself and also of Greenwood's work as an exposé of the scale of prevalence of homosexuality within the workhouse casual wards is compelling. Equally, the detective work uncovering the truths underpinning F. G. Wallace-Goodbody's 1883 'The Tramp's Haven' is really useful, and likewise the uncovering of Harry A. Franck's notebooks of his tramping travels.

REVIEW

It would be interesting to know where Seaber located another strand of the incognito social investigator – namely those who took to the road in disguise motivated by religious faith. The likes of Mary Higgs and the Rev. Jennings spring to mind as examples. Where do we locate such individuals, who had a campaigning concern for the homeless, into wider twentieth-century narratives about the importance of faith and social activism?

Finally, one aspect that I had hoped I might discover more about, but which did not feature in this volume beyond suggesting that the 'Peripatetic Journalist' of 1910 may have actually been a tramp (p. 48), was the emergence of a style of writing that I tend to think of as tramp advice manuals, which were written purportedly by anonymous tramps: Frank Stuart's *Vagabond*, Hippo Neville's *Sneak Thief on the Road* and Digit's *The Confessions of a Twentieth Century Hobo,* for example. How should we locate these against the autobiographical accounts of times spent tramping by the likes of Charlie Potter, Thomas Callaghan and Jim Phelan?

Overall, there is much of considerable interest in this volume. It deserves to be read, and for those with an interest in Orwell they will find his impact and legacy cropping up through the book.

Nick Crowson,
University of Birmingham

George Orwell Studies

Subscription information
Each volume contains two issues, published half-yearly.

Annual Subscription (including postage)

Personal Subscription

UK	£25
Europe	£28
RoW	£30

Institutional Subscription

UK	£100
Europe	£115
RoW	£120

Single Issue copies (subject to availability)

UK	£15
Europe	£17
RoW	£20

Enquiries regarding subscriptions and orders should be sent to:

> Journals Fulfilment Department
> Abramis Academic
> ASK House
> Northgate Avenue
> Bury St Edmunds
> Suffolk, IP32 6BB
> UK

Tel: +44(0)1284 700321
Email: info@abramis.co.uk

www.ingramcontent.com/pod-product-compliance
Lightning Source LLC
Chambersburg PA
CBHW080403170426
43193CB00016B/2795